The Poor Man's Road

to

Riches

The Poor Man's Road
to
Riches

Duane Newcomb

Parker Publishing Co., Inc.
West Nyack, N.Y.

Library of Congress Cataloging in Publication Data

Newcomb, Duane G
    The poor man's road to riches.

    Includes index.
    1. Success. 2. Finance, Personal.
I. Title.
HF5386.N37   650'.12   76-14910
ISBN 0-13-686717-0

Printed in the United States of America

What This Book Can Do for You

A real paradox exists in America today. On one hand the average man finds himself struggling harder than ever to make ends meet, while on the other hand thousands of "money-wise" fortune makers starting with rock-bottom salaries are cashing in on tremendous opportunities for real riches. Fortunately these big money opportunities are in no way confined to a select few. They are yours for the taking if you will simply reach out and grab them.

I originally discovered this fact and the principles and methods outlined in this book by accident. For several years I had been interviewing successful businessmen for a number of business magazines. One day I happened to talk to a former school teacher who owned a small trucking firm, several farms and a number of other enterprises grossing about fifteen million dollars a year. In the course of the conversation he explained that until a few years ago he had never made more than $9,000 a year, and that he and his wife had acquired their entire fortune utilizing the capital from his small yearly salary and a good plan. That was a startling revelation to me!

Then I realized that over the last few years I had interviewed at least a hundred successful fortune builders who had struck it rich over the same route. As I continued to interview I found hundreds more, all of whom started poor, but with a well-defined plan literally pulled themselves up by their bootstraps. I then sat down, analyzed what these people had done and put the details of the method into an organized plan.

That's what this book is all about. It is your step-by-step pre-tested guide for creating a giant fortune from your present income and other readily available money sources.

It starts you at rock-bottom circumstances . . . flat broke, deeply in debt, out of work . . . anywhere . . . and shows you exactly how to organize your life so that it propels you to riches.

The first half starts you in capital building immediately: it shows you how to estimate your capital building potential, gives you numerous automatic ways to take fortune-building capital from your present income, outlines ways to free up more fortune-building capital by selectively changing lifestyles, explains how to build your budget around your fortune-making activities, gives numerous tips for finding or creating extra capital-building jobs and offers sure-fire ways to borrow all you need to really get going.

The next five chapters show you exactly how to build a fortune with your created capital: they explain how to start a fortune-making business, how to create automatic habits that propel you to wealth, how to use ideas to multiply your fortune-making potential, how to get rich by being unconventional, and how to manage for giant riches.

The final chapter offers automatic investment opportunities that multiply your fortune many times with little personal effort. The book itself is extremely down to earth, and contains many concrete examples and illustrations that make your own fortune making practical. There are tips in every chapter that you can put to use immediately, along with steps to positive action that start you where you are right now and literally help propel you on to a big money income.

Duane Newcomb

Contents

The Poor Man's Road

to

Riches

1
How to Find Your Big Money Potential

We are living today in what might well be called the golden age of opportunity. Due to our tremendous technological advances each and every one of us has a far greater possibility of striking it rich than ever before. Look, for instance, at the potential of rapid transit, "people movers," cable TV, solar power and more. Every time science opens a new avenue or society's attitudes change, a whole new area of fortune-making opportunity opens up.

Strangely enough, however, many of the so-called "experts" keep telling us that the opportunity for great riches is today far smaller than it was many years ago.

It's true we don't have the Andrew Carnegies or the Henry Fords any more. But we do have the Lands, the Packards and the Lears—all men who've made tremendous fortunes from today's opportunities. So vast is the potential today that anyone who believes the chances for making it big are gone just doesn't understand what's really happening.

As John Paul Getty once said, "I never cease to be astounded by the prevalence of the negative attitude and in my opinion totally erroneous among supposedly intelligent people. There is a tremendous mass of evidence to prove that imaginative, resourceful and dynamic men have more opportunity to achieve wealth and success in business today than ever before in our history."

There is currently then a tremendous potential for anyone who wants to amass a giant fortune, but the money-making climate is far different than it used to be. Today might well be called the age of the millionaire who found a very specialized need and then filled it. A Seattle man, for instance, got rich helping other people market and promote their inventions. A New Jersey school teacher made a fortune providing real estate brokers all over the country with aerial photographs of land for sale, and a Miami factory worker parlayed a $300 investment into a million-dollar a year business providing gifts for people who couldn't seem to remember wives, relatives, friends, etc., at gift-giving time.

The Time Is Now

Like these millionaires and many others, you too can get rich if you really want to. The choice is up to you. You can say like some of the people that John Paul Getty talked to, that the chance to amass a fortune is gone, or you can realize that the world around you is always changing and that with every change come many additional opportunities to really clean up. The choice is up to you . . . Do you want to sit back and moan, or do you want to take the future in your hands and get started right now on your path to giant riches?

Free Yourself for Success Right Now

Conventional thinking says that a man making a small income will just never make it. Is this true? Absolutely not. Most people have tremendous potential. They have the ability to think up good useful ideas, the ability to get things done, the knack for making money, and a lot more. The one stumbling block that all of us run into, however, is what we call self-image. Scientists today have discovered that a man or a woman is exactly what he pictures himself to be. If you don't think you can do something, you can't—and that's where a lot of us get slowed down. As Harold Shuman, founder and president of EPS Research Associates Foundation, says in his book *How To Take Yourself Apart and Put Yourself Together Again,* you are what you have pictured yourself to be. But if you don't like the image that you're presenting to the world, that personality or identity, if you're not satisfied with the account you're giving of yourself right where you are at the moment, you can do much about this. This all-important concept (self-image) can make the difference between remaining where you are in an inadequate job forever or achieving something really worthwhile in life on your way to a giant fortune.

Randolph T., for instance, a 32-year-old Akron factory worker, found himself deeply in debt when his wife was in the hospital. Randolph decided, after reading several books on self-image psychology, that he had to do something now. He had thus far worked most of his life in a dull dead-end job because he had always believed that was all he was capable of doing. Once he understood the self-image problem, however, he realized he had lots of usable talents. His greatest strength was that he loved to talk to people, and people trusted him. Thinking this over he decided to try selling real estate. He then practiced seeing himself as a successful real estate agent: he visualized money changing hands, people signing contracts, and himself driving a new Lincoln Continental. At the end of his six-month image-building period he had received his real estate license and had arranged with a local real estate office to work four Saturdays a month.

The first month Randolph sold four properties and the second month, ten. He then quit his regular job and started selling full time. By the end of the first year he had made well over $34,000, had paid off all debts and was well on his way toward establishing his own real estate business and an even greater yearly income.

In another case Denny H., a 36-year-old Philadelphia school janitor, had been stuck in a mediocre dead-end job for almost ten years. Two days before his birthday, his wife took their two children and walked out, telling him she never wanted to see him again until he had made something of his life. For the first few days he simply sat around and brooded; then during the next week he began to talk to one of the teachers about his problem. This particular teacher explained that Denny really had a lot of ability he wasn't using and was probably his own worst enemy. Together they explored some of the valuable traits Denny had—the ability to organize, to see things that people needed, and to manage (he had organized a part-time group of students into a crackerjack crew that cleaned the school rapidly and well).

The teacher then got Denny to begin to see himself as more successful and to try to decide what he really wanted to do. After thinking it over Denny decided he'd like to go into his own business and that there was a great local need for a cheap supply of building materials for do-it-yourself homeowners. He also reasoned it would be easy for him to obtain these materials from buildings being torn down in nearby cities.

Before he actually began the business though, he began to prepare himself mentally. He visualized himself obtaining the materials, talking to customers, making sales, and in general creating a big success. At the end of four months he was ready to give it a try. He then took $600 from his savings account, rented a vacant lot, bought all the materials from an old building that was being demolished, set up a sign and started selling to the public at a good discount. Within eight months, Denny was making almost $3000 a month in profit. Two years later he opened three new locations, and today does a booming business that regularly grosses over $32 million a year.

All of this happened because both men had freed themselves from the idea that a man now making a small salary just doesn't have ability or the knowledge to make it big. If this is the state of mind you are now in, yet you have a desire to propel yourself to a big money fortune, it's time to start to improve your self-image right now.

Here are the steps:

1) Realize that you have many abilities you haven't used yet, some of which will help propel you toward your big money goals.

2) List seven things you do well (talking to people, making things with your hands, managing projects, etc.). Just put them down on a piece of paper.

3) Take ten minutes out every day and begin to see yourself as a successful person. Visualize yourself living in a big house, driving a big car, handling a big job, starting a business, and making money. Try to see yourself utilizing your better traits and personal habits. Within 20 to 45 days you will begin almost automatically to start seeing yourself as a success. When you reach this point you'll be ready to start off on your own path to great wealth.

How to Make Big Money By Creating Fortune-Building Capital

Once you have built your self-image to the point where you know you can do it, making big money then starts to become almost a science. There are certain rules, steps and procedures you can follow that will make you rich almost automatically. At this point, however, it's vitally important to concentrate on obtaining your basic fortune-building capital. Sometimes, of course, it's possible to start small with as little as $25 to $50 and build slowly—but this is the hard way. The more capital you can start with, the quicker you can be on your way to a giant fortune. In this book I'm first going to show you how with your own two hands (and little else except your own energy and the income you possess right now) you can easily build the capital you need to give yourself a really good start.

When you reach this point I'll give one warning—at all cost avoid the conventional thinking trap—*a man can never put together enough from his own income to really get started.* This is absolutely not true. Thousands of people have started with less than $10,000 a year income and within a year or two, utilizing only the basic capital-building methods easily available, have come up with $5000, $6000, $10,000 and even more to invest in their own business.

Bill R., for instance, a cannery worker making $7000 a year, decided that his dead-end job was getting him nowhere, and that if he was ever going to make it in life he had to strike out on his own. After much soul searching he decided because of the current home improvement boom, a small, nationally known carpet franchise would really pay off.

He needed $5000 as an initial investment, however. At that point Bill hadn't saved even one dollar toward the future. He reexamined himself thoroughly and decided that he just might make it. He then turned his spending habits upside down and started putting $300 in the bank every month before paying the other bills. He also managed to find a job on Sundays at a local gas station that brought him an extra $100 a month. Staying on this saving schedule was difficult, but by the end of the year he had put aside $4800. The rest he easily obtained from his local bank and immediately invested in the carpet franchise. Within five years he was grossing over $70,000 a year, and had acquired a large house in the country, a swimming pool and five cars.

There are many other examples: Raymond H., a St. Louis factory worker, making $10,000 a year, with a daughter to put through college, managed to save $4200 within a year's time, to make another $1500 on a part-time job and to borrow another $1000 for a total of $9,000 which he invested in his own rental equipment business. Today Ray has five businesses grossing over $1 million a year, a huge house, a mountain cabin and a plane which he flies to his various business locations.

Utilize These Big Money Capital Sources

Capital to launch your fortune-making activities is really extremely easy to acquire. In actuality all of us have a ready money tree that's out there waiting for us to simply take what we need. I know (if you're in debt or are spending every penny you make just for basic necessities) that what I'm saying just doesn't seem possible. That's because you aren't looking for your capital in the right places. If you are a working man with an average kind of job, the places to look for your fortune building capital are: *your present income, a second job,* and *borrowed money.* All three are equally important and will produce amounts that you never dreamed possible. Generally present income capital building and moonlighting go along together, and when you have created sufficient capital on your own, then it becomes as simple as ABC to borrow whatever else you need. Now let's look at each of these and see what possibilities exist.

Present Income

Present income, believe it or not, is a great investment capital source. Economists estimate that most of us squander a good 20% of our income without even realizing it. Most of us buy items we don't need, overpriced goods, frill services and more. In one university experiment, homeowners found they could easily save $3200 out of an $8000-a-year income by properly utilizing the money taken in. Today, while admittedly everything costs more, all of us have hidden fat that can be tapped if we know how. The problem is that if the money's available we generally find a place to spend every penny. Then when at the end of the month there isn't anything left, it's easy to convince ourselves that we've squeezed out every last bit of slack.

Moonlighting

Generally "moonlighting" is extremely important in your capital building program because it generally doubles the total amount you can accumulate and gives you an excellent tool when you're ready to borrow your remaining capital needs. It doesn't make a bit of difference what kind of moonlighting job you take because the main purpose is to add up that capital-building cash fast.

Creative fortune builders in the past have accumulated moonlighting capital working for a bicycle rent concession, mowing lawns on weekends, working as a part-time janitor, pumping gas on evenings and Sundays, etc. In this book we will show you how to moonlight effectively so you'll always get the most out of your fortune-building time.

Borrowed Capital

After you have put together $2,000, $3,000, $10,000 or more in fortune-building capital, and have a concrete plan for starting your fortune-building business, many banks and other sources will gladly lend you additional capital. The reason is that you have now given them something concrete they can actually invest in.

Dwight J., for instance, a former Philadelphia school teacher, who decided to try a neighborhood ice cream franchise, put together a $6000 nest egg and a franchising commitment, then approached his local banker for an additional $6,000. His plan looked so sound to the bank that he received the money within a few days, and opened for business the following month. His original business grew like "Topsy" until at the end of two years he had acquired five ice cream franchises, a five-figure income, two luxury cars and a large home in one of the better parts of town—all because he had learned how to effectively utilize the terrible trio of advanced capital building—*present income savings, moonlighting,* and *borrowed capital.*

How to Estimate Your Capital Building Potential

Just how do you estimate the amount of capital you can realistically accumulate? The method is easy: Even if you're in debt, or even if capital building looks hopeless, you can wind up with a good sized nest egg. Over the past twenty years, literally thousands of potential investors have proved time and time again that you can still take an extra 10 to 15% out of your present income if you just know how. To get a rough general idea (1) simply multiply your present income by 15 percent, (2) estimate moonlighting at an average minimum of $150 a month, and (3) figure you can realistically borrow 30 percent of what you're able to save from the other two sources.

If, for instance, you're now making $9000 a year, you will be able to take out around $1350 as income savings, $2400 by moonlighting, and another $1200 in borrowed capital for a total of $5000. With this you can start a great many fortune building businesses. And it is of course certainly possible to do better than this depending on the time and effort you're willing to put in.

So now let's go. Free yourself of the conventional thinking roadblocks, and let's get started here and now on your own road to a giant fortune.

POINTS TO REMEMBER

1. There is a tremendous potential today for anyone who wants to acquire a giant fortune.

2. Self-image is vital to your success: You can build your big money self-image this way:

    a. Acknowledge your hidden abilities

    b. List seven things you do well

    c. See yourself as the successful person you want to be for ten minutes every day.

3. You can acquire fortune building capital from:

    a. your present income

    b. a second job

    c. borrowed money

4. To estimate your big money capital building potential, multiply your present income by 15 percent, take $150 a month for the number of months you intend to moonlight, estimate you can borrow an additional 30 percent and add all three—present income savings, moonlighting, borrowed capital—together.

2
Automatic Methods That
Create Present
Income Cash Fast

Nearly every one of us today is caught in what I call the "up against the wall" illusion; that is, as we live life it seems to take every last penny just to keep up with the day-to-day expenses.

All costs have risen astronomically; food prices have exploded, clothing has skyrocketed, and everything else has shot up 10 percent to 200 percent and more.

All of this leads us to believe that we're working on such a tight budget now, that there's just no way to take out extra for our fortune-building activity. Even people who really should know better—college professors, bankers, economists—will tell you that the average man today has every bit of fat squeezed out of his paycheck and there's hardly anything at all left.

I have to admit that I thought this too for a long time; then one day I discovered I had been caught in the conventional thinking trap we talked about in the last chapter and had closed my eyes to the real possibilities around me. For a number of years I did magazine interviews with successful businessmen on how they'd become a success. One afternoon I was sitting in a kitchen in Modesto, California, talking to a young teacher and his wife, Donald and Betty R., about one of their businesses. Suddenly he stopped and said, "Do you really want to hear how we did this?" "Sure," I said. Then he began to talk:

Donald and Betty had gone along for several years just barely "squeezing by." One day they sat down and asked themselves if this was all they really expected out of life. The answer was no. They decided to literally turn their lifestyle upside down and go forward with the idea that at least a part of what they were now making could and should be utilized to make more money. At that time Donald was making $7000 a year; Betty, $6000. They decided that no matter what happened they were going to live on half of this and put the other half aside for their future businesss.

Although it was a real struggle, within two years they had saved $12,000, put a down payment on a truck, and hired a man to haul produce for local farmers on contract. In addition they bought 30 acres of grapes (with a small down payment) which they worked during the summer. Using this method they paid off the entire investment over the next four years and began to look around for other businesses. At this point, their income averaged about $75,000 a year and was increasing every month.

Over the years interviewing I have run into hundreds of other people who were bound and determined to pull themselves up by their own bootstraps, and literally carved their fortunes from their own incomes.

Bill T., for example, was a $9000-a-year Colorado bus driver, and deeply in debt. One afternoon he decided that there had to be a better way to live. He then began to keep a notebook in which he jotted down any idea he could think of that would enable him to take fortune-building capital out of his present income. Once he started, the number of methods he could dream up was surprising. Finally he stopped accumulating ideas and began to put them into practice. In some cases the methods needed to accumulate additional capital required Bill to completely reorient his lifestyle. This was a little difficult for the family but they agreed to go along for at least eight months. This was all Bill needed. And at the end of five months he had saved over $1800 which ballooned into a $4000 nest egg by the end of the first year. With that money he put a down payment on an old rooming house, which he sold three months later for a $3000 profit. He then took this money and bought two more rooming houses. He also put a down payment on a small tractor and back hoe, hired a man to operate it, and began renting it out to local contractors. When he sold the two houses a year later he again reinvested the money in a backpacking shop near one of Colorado's mountain resorts.

At the time I interviewed him, his income was approaching $100,000 a year, he lived in a beautiful house near Denver, and had become an extremely respected member of the business community.

These are just two cases, of course, but the more I interviewed the more I realized that not only was it possible to take fortune-building capital out of present income, but that there was a whole science of money income management that will work for anyone who's willing to incorporate the basic management principles in his daily life.

This Six-Step Method Can Make You Rich

After several years of analyzing successful present income capital builders I began to see that each had used six simple steps to actualize the big money potential in his own income.

These methods, while simple, have over the years turned out to be almost foolproof. Here are the steps:

Step 1: Make the decision that you intend to create a capital nest egg.

You must first make what you intend to do concrete and real. Once you decide what you want from yourself, put it down in black and white; that is, make a written promise to yourself:

I (whoever you are) am now making this decision on (put the date). I intend to create a capital nest egg of at least . . . . . . dollars. Then for the next few days, actually visualize this nest egg in your mind: See yourself holding it, counting it, etc. Once you become really associated with this money and it feels natural, then you're ready for the next step.

Step 2: Decide what percentage you want to take. You first need to decide how much cash you need at the end of six months or the end of a year. If you're making $8,000, for instance, you might want to say that at the end of a year you're going to take $2500 out of your present income. From a practical point of view that seems almost impossible. You must ignore that for now and simply decide how much you'll need. Now turn it into a percentage. Simply divide your yearly income ($8000) into the amount you wish to keep (in this case $2500). This is 31 percent of $8000, which is high. Fifteen percent is a good practical average. If you're really determined to take more and you feel it's practical, leave it at the first amount. Generally, however, anything over 25 percent is out of the question.

Step 3: Make out a budget including the amount you wish to pay yourself.

Now you've got to try to make the system really work. The first thing you must put on your monthly budget is the month's portion of that $2500 ($208). After that, add the rest of your expenses.

If you can't work the amount you want to save into your budget, then pare each flexible expense item down by 10 percent—food, recreation, vacation money, clothes, are flexible expenses; car payments, rent, etc. are generally fixed. You can also cut back on fixed expenses, but that generally requires a change in lifestyle. We'll take this up later.

Step 4: Pay yourself first and put it in the bank. Bill B., a $12,000-a-year St. Louis computer operator, found he could "practically" take out $120 a month he could use for capital building. Unfortunately, however, he just never seemed to be able to take the money. His wife wanted to go out to dinner, the children needed new shoes, he needed a new hose for the lawn—there was always something. A couple of times he managed to set aside $100, but generally it turned out to be $25 or less. At the end of the first year he'd only saved $350. This so disgusted him that he finally decided to take himself in hand and really do something. After that, on the first of each month he took the $120 and put it directly in the bank. No matter what happened after that, he forced himself to live on what was left. Once he had it in the bank he found he wasn't really tempted to spend it. This extra effort got the money for him in the first place and kept it intact from there on.

Step 5: Pay the rest of the bills only after you've taken out your fortune-building cash.

This is extremely important. When Bill first started putting the money in the bank, he'd sit down and pay his bills before he paid himself. In that way he was always tempted to pay a pressing bill and short cut his savings. Those bills will always be there. If you're on a cash saving program, pay yourself first and make the remainder cover the bills even if you have to split them up or carry some over.

If you have a doctor bill for $100, for instance, divide it into two $50 payments, or break it into $20 amounts and pay it out over a period of five months. You can't generally do this with long term fixed commitments, but flexible bills (like utilities) which are high one month and low the next can be juggled around. In addition, knowing you haven't paid the entire amount will almost automatically hold the next month's bill to a bare minimum.

Step 6: Don't dip into fortune-building cash for everyday living expenses.

As you begin to get in the swing of paying yourself first, you'll suddenly discover sometime during the month that you need more money for groceries, kids' shoes, or something similar. There's the money in the bank; at this point it's a great temptation to use it. Don't ... or it will begin to drain away. Simply keep your eye on the amount you'll have in the bank at the end of the year. Just keep reminding yourself that you will soon need this cash—all of it—for your fortune-building activities.

Automatic Methods That Build Cash Fast

You can, if you like, take your capital-building cash out of your paycheck every month and deposit it personally in the bank, but that's the hard way. The best, easiest, and most effective method is to pick some automatic system that, once started, builds regularly every month without any additional handling.

Fred J., for instance, decided he needed at least $3200 by the end of the year to take over an ice cream-hamburger franchise at a local resort area. Utilizing the six-step method, Fred, a Memphis factory worker, began to take out of his paycheck every month $266 which he then deposited in the bank. All went fine for the first couple of months, and then he began to hold out small amounts for needed expenses (groceries, tires, dentist bills, etc.). As the months went by the amounts he deposited in the bank grew smaller and smaller. It was at this point he realized that if his capital saving program continued like that he would fail miserably. The only solution was to take the money handling out of his hands entirely. He then opened a checking account (which he'd never had before) and authorized the bank to take $266 out each and every month for deposit in his capital building account. After that his big money capital building proceeded smoothly and painlessly. Nine months later he had put aside the entire $3200, borrowed an additional $2200 from the local bank and launched the ice cream-hamburger franchise. Within two years his original unit grew to 12, while his take-home income skyrocketed to $55,000 a year . . . all because he'd been smart enough to make his big money savings plan automatic.

Here are more methods to try:

Make Your Boss Your Key to Money Power

Your boss, if you'll let him, can be your key to giant riches. Not every company, of course, will take money out of your paycheck each month and send it to your savings account, but some will. The advantage is you'll never know it's gone and will quickly grow accustomed to living on the smaller amount. A great many fortune builders have used this method as their path to great riches. Colin T. of Boston, for instance, a $9000 a year janitorial service worker, tried time and time again to save money to open a small cabinet shop. Several years went by, however, and he wasn't one penny nearer his goal. Then one afternoon while discussing the problem with a couple of friends, they asked why he didn't simply ask his boss to send the money to the bank every payday. In that way he'd hardly know it was gone. The first month he felt the loss; the second month he and his wife fared a bit better. After that, however, they began to adjust. At the end of the year, utilizing all three capital-building methods—present income, moonlighting, and a capital loan—Colin managed to accumulate $10,000. He then invested the money with a partner in a small shop. Colin insisted from the beginning on high quality and low prices. As a result, within the first five months custom builders began to seek him out, and within two years the business itself had expanded until there were nine employees and a yearly gross income of over $700,000. At this point Colin bought himself two limousines, a complete new wardrobe for himself and his wife, and a large vacation cabin in Maine.

Take the Bank Route To a Giant Fortune

This method is easy but extremely effective. Simply open a checking and a savings account and authorize the bank to deposit a given amount into your savings account every month. This may seem overly simple, but this one step alone will create big money capital almost automatically where everything else has failed.

Let Stocks Build Your Fortune

Here's a new method and a fascinating one. Stocks aren't new, of course, but until recently you had to deal almost exclusively with a stock broker to buy stocks. Now many banks offer the small investor a chance to buy some stocks automatically. Simply authorize the bank to invest from $20 to $500 every month from your checking account. They then automatically invest for you in any or all of the top 25 stocks ranked by value of shares outstanding on the Standard and Poor's 425 Industrial Index. The advantage: you save fees because the bank makes block purchases. During a period when stocks go up, your investment not only makes money from the savings program itself but the stocks will increase in value and when you're ready to cash out they generally will be worth more than you paid in the beginning.

Commit Yourself to a Mutual Fund

If you don't like stocks you can make a mutual fund your automatic escalator to fortune-building capital. A mutual fund, of course, is simply an investment company formed by a large number of people to pool their money to invest in stocks and other securities. With some companies you can simply authorize your boss to send part of your paycheck every month to the mutual fund of your choice. Today of course you have a wide selection. You have a choice of the so-called go-go and basic funds. Go-go funds are simply funds that play the market for the highest possible stakes. Unless you're willing to risk a loss or two, it's best not to try these. With a basic fund you still have a good choice. There are such things as growth funds, growth with income funds, income with growth funds, so-called balance funds, and income funds. A good middle ground when you're trying to raise a capital nest egg as we are is the income fund. It will probably give you the largest return in the shortest time. You can get information on these by calling any stockbroker listed in the telephone yellow pages. The following books will give you additional detailed information about mutual funds:

- *What About Mutual Funds?* John Straley, Harper and Row, 1967.

- *Understanding Investments and Mutual Funds,* G.W. Potts, Arco, 1973.

Make Your Home a Big Money Gold Mine

Believe it or not, your own home is still the best big money leverage tool that you have available. Take a closer look . . . it's an automatic nest egg that you must invest in every month. It accumulates principal regularly, and the value continues to go up—without you lifting a finger. In addition, if you've lived there for some time you probably already have a good size equity available for use. Roger G., for instance, a $9000-a-year Chicago factory worker who had been severely crippled in an accident and needed money badly, just couldn't get started on any savings plan. Sitting at home one evening, however, he suddenly realized that he really had a big money bonanza in his own home that he'd been investing in all along. Next morning he walked into a local bank, borrowed $5000 against the accumulated equity and three weeks later opened a small waterbed shop in a growing section of town. This was just about the beginning of the waterbed boom. At the end of the first year Roger had taken out a cool $35,000 profit, and the next year he grossed well over $300,000. He is currently on Easy Street, with a number of additional businesses producing income.

If this method appeals to you there are two ways to go. You can sell your home outright to raise capital (in which case you'll have to rent somewhere) or you can borrow against your equity. That, of course, means a pay back payment every month. Now sit down and look at what it's actually going to cost.

Say you're now living in a $30,000 house and your payments are $225 a month. The house is increasing in value at about $2000 a year or $167 a month and you are accumulating about $35 a month in equity. To rent the same home somewhere else would cost you $275 . . . $50 more than you are now paying. Now add it all up:

additional cost to rent	$ 50
loss in increased value	167
loss in accumulated equity	35
total cost to you	$252 a month

On the other hand, suppose you have a $15,000 equity in this house and you want to borrow $5000 against it. Many lending institutions will let you borrow $5000 with a five-year payback at 18 percent interest . . . $126.96 a month payback. Borrowing would cost you $25 more a month out of pocket than if you sold and rented somewhere else, but if you sold, you'd also be losing $202 a month in equity and value increase—not really much of a choice if you can afford to make the loan payments out of your present income. If you can't, however, selling will give you the money you need for your big money fortune building.

**Buy a Government Bond and Increase Your
Big Money Potential**

Simply authorize your employer to take a bond out of your paycheck each month. This is an old tried-and-true method that millions of Americans have utilized successfully for years. Bonds pay 5 3/4 percent interest. Investing $100 every month for a year would give you an additional $37.44 at the end of that year. Many present income capital builders prefer this method over all others because most large companies are already set up to make payroll deductions for bonds. For instance, a $8500-a-year Kansas City factory worker, Gerald R., was deeply in debt to pay off his wife's hospital expenses, but he had long wanted to run his own business. One evening he and his wife were talking about starting a small real estate business when she reminded him that he was already accumulating big money capital in the company payroll deduction bond program that could be used for this purpose. He then started studying real estate evenings and at the end of that year cashed in the bonds for an accumulated total of about $1800, borrowed $1800 against his own home and went to work for a real estate office in a small rural community. A year later he opened his own office which prospered almost immediately. Shortly after that Gerald bought a thousand-acre ranch nearby, built the family a five-bedroom home with a swimming pool, and bought his own plane in which to fly clients around the county. If you're looking for an easy way to accumulate capital then you should consider this method.

**Smart Money Shortcuts That Create
Even More Capital**

From now on if you're really serious about fortune building you should constantly be on the lookout for additional ways to accumulate big money capital. The criteria: they should be easy, painless, and almost automatic. Here are several offbeat methods to consider:

1. *Sell what you already own*

This isn't a new or different method but it's effective. Everyone has clothes, bookends, old lamps and other odds and ends they no longer need which can be used to raise capital. This fits our capital building requirements well since you have little additional cost and little additional effort. Ralph B. was a $11,000-a-year California railroad worker with a family of nine and a growing debt load. He nevertheless decided he'd like to try a novelty fast food hamburger operation in which the customers cooked their own hamburgers. Unfortunately by the time he got ready to launch the business he was still $500 short. The next two weeks Ralph tried several ways to raise the additional capital without luck. One day as he was putting the car in the garage he began looking at some of the items stored there: three old lamps, four candle holders, two unusual old chests, etc. He realized that almost all of it was saleable. That night he put a garage sale ad in the paper, set up two large signs at either end of the block, moved everything to the middle of the garage and tagged each piece with the asking price. By the end of the weekend he had taken in exactly $585, more than enough to launch his new enterprise. By the end of that year his novel hamburger operation had really caught on, so he opened three more. These did so well that Ralph B. had soon cleared $50,000 above all expenses. He then moved his family to a new home, put in a swimming pool, and bought each family member their own individual sports car.

To start, simply advertise particular items in newspaper classified sections, or run a garage sale. Advertise this with ads in the classified, signs on the lawn, and signs at either end of the block leading to your house. These methods are currently extremely popular and generally raise considerable cash.

2. *Consider selling that second car*

Here's an all-American cash-building method that few of us consider. In this day of affluent America many of us have a second car that really gets very little use, or (if you live in the city) an only car that we could eliminate by relying on public transportation. When trying to raise cash for your fortune-building activities, remember that any car (sitting most of the time in your garage) actually represents money. It also meets the other criteria for our capital-building shortcuts since in many cases it's already paid for and the cash accumulation is all automatic. Consider the payments you've made in the same light as putting money in the bank.

To convert your car into cash, simply run an ad in the local paper under "automobiles," stating the type, price, condition, and any other selling features. Even if your car isn't completely paid for, you can still sell it, pay off the loan and keep the difference between what you owed and the selling price to invest in your fortune-building activities.

3. *Purchase land as a short term investment.*

Most people buy land to use or as a long term investment, but it's also possible to use it as a quick easy capital raising method. Today it's possible to purchase second-hand vacation lots or other small parcels for a few hundred dollars down and small monthly payments. This type of investment almost automatically puts pressure on you to make payments. In addition, besides building up equity, the value of this kind of investment grows five to 30 percent a year. These investments can be found in newspaper classifieds, in magazine classifieds, in such magazines as *Field and Stream* and *Mechanix Illustrated.* When you're ready to utilize this money, you can usually resell with an ad in the local newspaper.

4. *Consider your retirement plan.*

This probably is a last-ditch method since generally you want to keep your retirement plan intact. Some companies, however, allow your invested retirement plan money to be taken out in cash. When you're considering your own future, remember that this source can sometimes be tapped and should be considered along with all the other methods.

BASIC POINTS TO REMEMBER

1. Despite the up-against-the-wall illusion it is possible to take big money capital out of your present paycheck.

2. Utilize the six-step method to build capital from present income.

    a. Make the decision to create a capital nest egg.

    b. Decide what percentage (or amount) you want to take.

    c. Make out a budget . . . include what you wish to pay yourself.

    d. Pay yourself first.

    e. Pay bills after you've taken out your fortune-building cash.

    f. Don't dip into fortune-building cash for every-day living expenses.

3. Build cash automatically in these ways.

    a. Authorize your company to send money to your bank every payday.

    b. Authorize the bank to transfer money to your savings account every payday.

    c. Sign up for a bank stock plan.

    d. Sign up for a mutual fund plan.

    e. Obtain money by selling your home or borrowing against it.

    f. Sign up for the government bond payroll plan.

3

Magic Secrets That Multiply Your Capital Building Potential

You can without a doubt accumulate all the fortune-building capital you'll ever need almost automatically, utilizing the big money methods presented in the last chapter. But taking money from your present income, no matter how painlessly it's done, puts additional strain on your budget.

At least that's the way it is for the average man today. Fortunately, however, it isn't really necessary to suffer simply to take 15 to 20 percent from your present paycheck every month. After all, you can easily cut one third off your present living expenses and never notice the difference. The basic problem is that most of us live in a way that literally gulps money (in most cases needlessly). After all, as mentioned before, there are people in the U.S. today that manage reasonably well on $1200 to $5000 a year. In this chapter, then, we want to learn the secrets of cutting down painlessly so (1) you will have no difficulty taking out whatever big money capital you decide to save and (2) you can free up even more money to utilize in your fortune-building activities.

How to Create More Fortune-Building Capital

The only real way to create more fortune-building capital from your present income, naturally, is to cut down the amount you spend. Unfortunately, simply using "will power" to cut back is almost impossible since most of us need every penny just to cover day-to-day living expenses.

Take a closer look at the average family, however, and you'll discover that many expense items we now take for granted are not really necessary. Once eliminated, these items will not only "free up" available investment cash, but will actually make life simpler, happier, and in some cases more healthful.

A second car, for instance, often appears to be a necessity, but there are many advantages in eliminating it. Daily schedules become less clogged as we learn to let children take the bus or car pool and to group shopping chores for evenings and weekends. Needless to say, not purchasing a second car in the first place frees cash ordinarily used for regular monthly upkeep and for the initial investment.

There are also many advantages in not buying packaged convenience foods from the supermarket. These refined foods are generally less nutritious than cheaper, more natural ones, and are also often spiked with harmful chemicals. Eliminating these will give the family a more healthful diet and at the same time produce substantial savings that can be plowed back into your individual investment activities.

The same principles also apply to such luxuries as throwaway diapers, kitchen gadgets, and many other special services.

The real secret of freeing up more fortune-building capital, then, is to selectively change lifestyle so that you retain the essential necessities, yet cut back on wasteful income gulpers. Take the case of Jim J., for instance, a Philadelphia carpenter. He wanted to take $3000 out of his $13,000-a-year income, so he began to reexamine his budget carefully. Soon he realized that his wife frequently picked out the most expensive items on the grocery shelf: peach jam at $1.20, for instance, when an 89¢ jar of the same size would do, or 48¢ for a brand name can of peas when the store had the same size available at 32¢. He himself had just bought a set of tools for $62.00 when he could have gotten by with the $49.99 quality. He then sat down and listed 61 purchases over the last three months they could have cut down. After that he made up a list of expense priorities, got the family together and talked to them about how they could live differently and wind up with extra cash to invest in their own future. They agreed and easily saved $3000 the first year and $4000 the second. Taking this $7000 as capital, they invested in a cut-rate carpet shop in a Northern California community. The shop did well from the very first and at the end of the second year was grossing well over $30,000.

Now here are the lifestyle areas that will help you accumulate more wealth-building cash:

Get Yourself Really Worked Up

Getting yourself really worked up is not a lifestyle change, but it will tremendously effect your entire life. Great wealth comes to those who have the *power* to attract it. In analyzing thousands of cases of people who have gone from poverty to great riches, I have learned that the power that has taken them there is simply the great determination they built in their own mind. What you must do is take your desire to be rich and make that desire grow until it becomes a strong burning force which nothing can stop.

Five years ago James B., for instance, found himself driving a five-year-old car, living in a poor neighborhood, and holding down a dead-end power company job. Gradually it dawned on him that if he didn't do something about his own situation, it would never change. The more he thought about it the more it bothered him. At first it was just annoyance, then it became a restless force, and finally his desire to change and start down the path to great riches grew so strong he could almost taste it. For three weeks he kept going over and over his desire to make money until he was a seething inferno. At the end of that time he marched into his boss's office, quit his job, went straight to the bank and asked for a $20,000 loan. At first the banker refused him, but James told him that no matter what the initial answer he was going to get that loan if he had to come back every day for the next five years. The banker simply said no on the first three days. On the fourth day the banker refused to see him; on the fifth he was forcefully removed by a bank guard; on the sixth day the police were called, but on the seventh day the banker agreed to at least listen to his entire plan instead of just saying no. At that point James laid out his plan for renovating old houses and turning them into nursing homes for older people. After listening to his entire plan and seeing his determination, the banker agreed to a loan for the initial project. The first nursing home was ready to go within four months and proved extremely successful. Within a year James opened two more which eventually grew to a string of 15. At this point he was personally making $72,000 a year, had a luxury home on a nearby lake and over $50,000 in the bank. All of this happened because he built his desire into a strong irresistible power that simply overwhelmed everything in its path.

Napoleon Hill, in his book *Think and Grow Rich,* (Fawcett) gives one formula for creating a burning desire; here I want to give you another. (1) Make the decision that you want to be rich (we've talked about this before). (2) Start becoming emotionally involved with that decision. Visualize yourself with a barrelful of money. Reach down; grab it; throw it up in the air; grab it some more; visualize yourself continually acquiring money. (3) Get tense about it. Go off by yourself somewhere for ten minutes a day and start working yourself up. First keep telling yourself, "I want money." Next demand money; then start shouting at the top of your voice, "I want money; I want money." Finally let yourself go physically. Take a rolled up newspaper and start hitting the back of a chair violently, screaming, "I want money."

Though all this may seem unnecessary the object is to take that emotional power within you and turn it into a burning desire that will act as an automatic motor to run over each and every obstacle between you and a giant fortune.

Get Off the Credit Gimmick

America today runs on credit. It is currently possible to buy appliances, vacations, golf clubs and anything else on monthly payments. Credit itself has become a huge industry, with almost 55 million credit cards in circulation at the end of 1973. Most Americans, of course, are willing to pay for the convenience of buying now and paying in installments later. Fortunately this phenomena provides you with a golden opportunity for creating even more big money capital out of your own paycheck. If you are currently operating on bank card credit, you are paying at least 18 percent in interest charges, and sometimes more. In addition, it's an established fact that people utilizing credit cards tend generally to buy 30 percent more merchandise than those who pay all cash. To increase your big capital building potential, then, the first lifestyle change you must make is to get off credit and save that extra money for your own pocket.

Most financial counselors agree that an average family of four living on a $10,000-a-year income pays roughly $212 a year in interest charges (exclusive of house payments). All of this money could go in your own pocket.

Now let's look at the credit purchases of a typical family:

	Payments	*Credit Charges*
Revolving charge	$ 25.00	$ 3.00
Refrigerator	18.00	2.67
Automobile	85.00	26.67
Personal loan	60.00	12.00
		$ 44.34

As you can see, then, every month this family literally throws away $44.34 in credit charges—money they could use for creating their own great fortune. Since an automobile requires a great deal of money, you may well not have enough cash available for this. But you can immediately begin to get off the credit habit with most other purchases and once off, stay off permanently. Here's how to do it:

1. Make a list of all the various credit accounts you are now utilizing (make it complete). This will make you aware of the extent to which you're utilizing this money-draining crutch.

2. Cut up and throw away all credit cards—oil company cards, department store cards and all others.

3. Stop charging on any other type of account. You may, of course, run into emergencies which force you to buy on credit (illness, unforseen expenses, etc.) but from now on you should use credit only to make money—not to incur personal debt.

4. Pay cash for any item you do buy. If you don't have the cash, put off buying until you do. This may be hard at first, but you must do it if you ever expect to escape the credit trap.

5. Pay off old accounts as best you can. You must pay living expenses first before old bills. If you don't have enough money left over to do this, do what you can. It is much more important to stop charging new items than to pay off old ones. Your creditors may be unhappy with this policy, but you're trying to make yourself rich, not them. Remember: you come first—*nobody else.*

By following these rules you will gradually change to a non-credit way of life—and will eventually free this money for your own productive big money purposes.

Make Money Paying Cash

Besides adding to your fortune-building capital by slashing credit charges, it's also possible to add to your fortune-building funds while paying cash.

There are today several card programs offering cash discounts. One of the best known is United International Club Inc., P.O. Box 3485, Beverly Hills, California 90212. This particular plan, UNIC, has over 1,000 member stores and restaurants in the Los Angeles area alone that offer discounts as high as 40 percent for paying cash.

Bill T., for instance, had ambitions of owning his own string of record shops. Bill managed to lay aside over $300 in a short period by depositing the savings from his card. Each time he made a purchase and received a discount, he put that savings in a box to be later deposited in the bank. This amount, added to his other savings at the end of a year and a half, gave him more than enough capital to begin business. Within two years Bill's first shop had expanded to seven which today produce slightly over $700,000 in gross income.

The Secrets of Making a Profit Out of Every Meal

Believe it or not, meal time can be your big profit time. Many home economists feel that most families waste more money grocery shopping than anywhere else. By altering our food buying and eating habits slightly, it's quite possible to utilize that extra money to build our own big money fortunes.

Rick H., for instance, a Chicago factory worker who had ambitions to enter the water bed business, decided maybe he could save some of the $80 a week his family spent on food for their fortune-building activities. Basically they cut out frills, made an extensive search for the cheapest stores, and generally tried to spend 15 percent less every week for food. To their surprise, they lopped off almost 20 percent the first three months and from 20 to 25 percent after that. By the end of the year they accumulated $600 from this one source alone.

Today there are generally three major ways in which you can make money from your food budget:

By Changing Lifestyles

Many of the foods we buy today have little real food value yet can really run up the food bills. The first step: cut out all frills and buy only those products that really feed the family.

Here are some tips I have put together from interviews with over 100 expert food buyers that will help you keep more of your food dollar.

1) Buy food only in a grocery store. Foods bought at hamburger stands, sandwich trucks, drive-ins, etc. cost twice as much.

2) Don't buy presliced meats or cheese. The slicing and packaging can more than double the price per pound.

3) Never buy canned baby food. Babies can and will eat all kinds of food simply mashed up.

4) Never buy soda or candy. This alone can save you $50 to $100 in a year's time.

5) Don't eat out of cans. Canned vegetables are relatively tasteless compared to fresh ones and cost much more. They may be more convenient, but you're going to pay for it.

6) Don't buy convenience foods, (individual tea bags, packaged rice dishes and similar items). You'll save at least 20 percent if you buy foods in bulk.

Save Money Shopping

Besides making sure your money really goes for good substantial food, you can also save 10 percent to 20 percent of the amount you now spend for food by shopping properly. Here are some tips:

1) Watch the ads for meat specials. Meat is the most expensive item that you buy, so shop in the supermarket that offers the best specials. Don't concentrate on one supermarket; keep switching around.

2) Shop the "new" warehouse supermarkets. These food warehouses offer merchandise out of crates and require you to do your own bagging. The warehouse also offers fewer brands and sizes, reducing inventory. A family can save 5 to 10 percent a week just by warehouse shopping.

3) Avoid supermarkets that give trading stamps and those that offer services such as babysitting.

4) Always look for mispriced items. Many claim they always find several mispriced items on each shopping trip (cans retailing for 50¢ can frequently be marked 05¢, for instance).

Cash In On Coupon Promotions

Believe it or not, coupon promotions are extremely important to your big money fortune-building plans. These may seem like peanuts, but cash offers by companies today add up to 4.5 to 6 billion dollars a year. Followed meticulously, these offers can actually cut a family food budget in half. Two kinds of offers are available today: 1) Cents-off redemption slips that you take into the store for an immediate discount, and 2) cash refunds you obtain by sending in part of the product box. These add up to far more than you realize. Say, for instance, you buy a package of 89¢ biscuits with a coupon which you turn in for 15¢. The biscuits now cost 74¢. You then send the package end to the company and receive a 50¢ refund. The biscuits have now cost you 24¢ (minus 13¢ postage) for a savings of 52¢. This is still not much, but considering the many offers available at any one time, collecting two a day will result in a yearly bonus of over $395.

You'll find these offers in daily newspapers, in magazines, on supermarket bulletin boards and in junk mail.

There are 12 companies that make regular refund offers: Best Foods, Borden, General Mills, General Foods, Green Giant, Kraft, Lever Brothers, Pillsbury, Proctor and Gamble, Standard Brands, and Stokeley.

Veteran refunders save as many product boxes of these 12 companies as they can find because they always mean money in the bank. Some refunders ask friends to save boxes for them; others go to laundromats for soap containers, and still others rummage the city dump. To keep track of what's being offered at any one time, you can subscribe to one of the following refund bulletins:

1) *Golden Opportunities,* Box 262, Hannibal, Ohio 43931

2) *Money Tree,* Box 39, Valley Park, Mo. 63008 ($1)

3) *Refund Round-Up* 548 W. Graisbury, Audubon, N.J. 08106 (50¢)

4) *The Refunder,* Box 888, Manhattan Beach, Calif. 90266 (50¢ per issue)

5) *The Firefly Reporter,* Box 95, Westbrook, Minn. 56183 (60¢ per issue)

How To Bargain Your Way to a Giant Fortune

There is, if you look for it, hidden big money capital in everything you buy. You won't accumulate anything if you continue present spending habits, of course. But by deciding to take your future in your own hands and ignoring conventional ways of living, it's possible to turn your present income into a big money gold mine.

For instance, Sheridan H., a $8000-a-year Los Angeles retail store clerk, was trying to put together enough capital to open a poodle grooming service. Sheridan was constantly searching for new ways to divert money from everyday living expenses for use in his capital building program. He was at one point regularly putting aside $97 a month, but Sheridan was extremely impatient. While going over his budget one evening he suddenly realized that every month the family bought a number of items: groceries, clothes, school supplies and tools, for which they paid the full retail price without a question. This, he reasoned, represented a potential additional amount that could be added to the fund.

During the next month he and his wife bought a washing machine, he purchased a set of automotive wrenches, and together they regularly bought fruit and vegetables to feed the family.

This time, instead of accepting the offered price, Sheridan did the following: he offered the appliance store $50 less than the tag price for the washing machine—and was accepted. He looked in the classified section of the local paper for the wrenches he wanted, then offered $35 less—and again was accepted. Finally he and his wife shopped at the local farmers' market for fresh fruits and vegetables, offering from 5 to 10 percent less per pound than what was being asked.

During the next six months Sheridan estimated they saved at least $300 utilizing the bargaining technique. At the end of this time he then took this money along with $5000 put together from other sources and opened his grooming service in a small store front in a fashionable section of town. It proved so popular that Sheridan soon had six more shops and a $35,000-a-year personal income. He then moved into a luxury apartment near his first shop and took the entire family on a trip to Europe as a bonus for their effort in helping build the family fortune.

Nearly every large city has some place, usually an open air market, where people set up booths to sell all sorts of merchandise—auto tools, furniture, rugs, food, etc. Not only are the prices at such markets generally low, but the booth proprietors are usually open to haggling over price. You can offer whatever you want to pay and it's up to the proprietor to accept or reject your offer. Armed with prices from the discount store you're ready to really start making big money. Simply offer 20 percent less than the discount price for whatever you intend to buy. Generally you'll haggle over this, but if you can settle for 10 percent off you're still ahead. Suppose, for instance, you want to buy a hand saw priced at $6.50 at the local discount store. If you buy it at 10 percent off, you save 65¢. In a year this method can add another $300 to $400 to your big money fortune-building fund. Although each method taken individually is fairly insignificant, all together they add up to an extremely large big money clout.

Next get yourself a box (or a small bank) and set aside all savings. If, for instance, you saved 65¢ on the saw, you must immediately take that money out of your pocket and put it in the box. Remember—if you had bought that particular item from the discount store you would have spent that additional amount anyway. You must set it aside, however; otherwise (if you're like the rest of us) you will probably spend it before it can be used for your big money fortune building.

Barter For Everything

Bartering can also add extensively to your big money fortune-building cash. Undoubtedly you have many items you never use that could be very useful to somebody else, and which you can trade for something you do need. Suppose, for instance, you need a new refrigerator and you're able to spend $10 a month for it. If you go out and buy a refrigerator, that $10 goes into somebody else's fortune-building activities. Suppose, however, you have a small old outboard motor that you never use sitting in your garage. How about trading that for a refrigerator? Simply put an ad in the newspaper, or place a notice on the local supermarket bulletin board. Chances are you'll quickly find somebody who wants to trade. You can't stop here, however. That $10 you could afford to spend must now go into your big money fortune-building fund. (Just put it in the bank on the first of every month). I'm not trying to teach you how to live cheaply but how to create big money fortune-building capital out of your present income and how to put it aside for actual fortune building.

Do It Yourself To Create a Big Cash Potential

Today we've almost completely relinquished control over our basic needs—food, clothing, shelter, and many others. As a result we pay out tremendous amounts of money to other people for services we used to perform ourselves: home repairs, yard upkeep, plumbing, etc., which unfortunately limits our ability to acquire fortune-building capital. People who know how to control these expenditures frequently free up considerable fortune-building capital. James T., for instance, spent many years just barely scraping by. When James decided to go into business for himself, however, he began to look for ways to acquire capital. He managed to immediately start taking $100 a month out of his present income and add another $60 a month from a part-time job. This wasn't enough, however, so James began to look for places where he could change his regular spending habits and accumulate additional fortune-building capital. He realized that during the past year he had paid a plumber $70, an electrician $120 and a carpenter $160—a total of $350. James then resolved to handle this kind of work himself from then on and add this money to his fortune-building capital. Over the next year he added $200 from this source, $350 from other lifestyle changes, $1200 from present income, $720 from a second job, and $4000 from a local lending source. He then took the $6470 and put a down payment on a small singles bar in New York City. This one did so well that he opened three more within six months. At the end of four years he was taking home over $70,000 a year and owned a large home on Long Island and several luxury cars.

To plug this big money capital leak then you should

resolve to do as much as possible for yourself instead of hiring someone to do it. Make yourself a home fix-up kit with a hammer, screw-driver, pliers, saw, pipe wrench, crescent wrench, small wood plane, medium-size file, hacksaw, wood chisel, putty knife, paint brush and oil can, plus electrical tape, jars of assorted nails, screws, Duco Cement, white glue, Bargo glue, plastic and mending cement, and waterproof resinol glue (for use on furniture). In this way you can tackle many jobs. What we're trying to do, of course, is to channel money you would ordinarily use and can afford to spend into your own big money fortune-building activities.You must first utilize this avenue only if you can afford it, and second, immediately take out whatever you would have paid someone else and place it in the bank. (You can, of course, also pay yourself on the install-ment plan.) If you can't afford to do this at any particular time, put it off, since the main object is to build big money capital.

Get Rich By Destroying the Income Gulpers

The more income gulpers you can get rid of, the more you can channel that money into fortune-building activities. You should learn to recognize them and destroy them relentlessly. There are five major ones you'll want to attack. Let's take a look at them and see what we can do:

1) *Late Payment Fees*

Late fees in themselves don't seem important, but if you are one of those millions who have the habit of paying a little late (and acquiring late fees) the total amount can really creep up on you. Bill F., for instance, always had payments to make on a car, on furniture or on his house, and while he always paid he sometimes got as much as two months behind. As a result he paid late payments every year. He simply shrugged this off as inconsequential until one day he added it up and realized that that particular year he had paid $120 in late fees, all money that he could use to launch his own business. Disgusted, he decided to stop this drain completely. He had been allowing someone else to take his money needlessly to use for their fortune building—not his.

If you've gotten into this habit and you're determined to build your own big money fortune, take steps immediately to stamp it out. After all, there's absolutely no reason why you should give money away when you can use it for your own purposes.

2) *Overpayment for necessities*

You certainly never overpay for necessities, right? Don't be so sure. Practically everybody does, but it's a real waste of your big money potential.

A Seattle factory worker, James McV., used to complain to his wife that they couldn't save money. He had never had any spare money to launch the picture framing business he'd always dreamed of starting. One day he stepped back and took a careful look at the budget. After thinking it over, he realized he and his wife could have easily saved $2 to $3 on every item they had purchased in the last two months. For instance, they had just bought a brand-name iron for $19.95. Two days later James found the same iron for $3 less at a discount drug store. The same was true of many other items. Adding it up, he realized that in the last two months they had thrown away $42 that he could have invested in his framing business. After that the family visited or called four or five stores before they bought anything, and nearly always managed to save $2 to $3 on each item. At the end of the year he put aside over $400 previously given away to other people.

If you intend to plug this loophole in your own spending habits, then it is important to always try to find the best bargain, not pay more than you have to for any particular piece of merchandise, and then, as before, immediately place that savings in the bank to help increase your fortune-building capital.

3) *Special Fees*

Bill J., a Chicago school teacher, wanted badly to begin a riding stable in the area where he lived. Yet he could never seem to get out of debt, let alone accumulate fortune-building capital. In looking over his own income, however, Bill found there were many areas he could tighten up. One area he found especially obnoxious was that of special fees. He had, for instance, paid $4 for a discount house membership, $3 in retouching fees to a local photography firm, and $2 to a car rental agency for insurance. The yearly total of these fees came to almost $95, money that really produced nothing yet could have been used as part of his riding stable capital. Plugging this loophole and several others during the following year, Bill managed to accumulate $900 from these sources, $2000 from present income, $900 from a second job and $3000 from a local lending institution. With this money, he put a down payment on a nearby riding academy; the remainder of the price was carried by the owner. Over the next five years, utilizing similar sources, he purchased five more businesses which netted him $42,000 a year in personal income.

If you are plagued by special fees, then, simply cut them relentlessly. The rule is to look at each item you're asked to pay for and determine if it offers something you can't do without. If it doesn't, eliminate it immediately and utilize this money for your own capital building.

4) *Impulse Purchases*

Retail establishments know they can entice people into buying more than they intended to by displaying items so attractively that people buy on impulse. Some point-of-purchase experts become so good they can sell $100, $200, or $300 items on the basis of sight alone. Supermarkets are especially guilty of utilizing mass impulse purchase psychology. Notice the huge bulging baskets of batteries, razor blades and fancy dishes stacked in a modern supermarket. These are impulse items you are expected to buy while grocery shopping. If you really need them, fine; but if it's just something you pick up because it's there, you're wasting your money. One potential capital builder estimated his family spent $7 or $8 for impulse purchases on every grocery trip for a total of $390 a year—money he could certainly use for starting his fortune-building business.

If impulse spending is plaguing you, first become aware that you or your family is spending money impulsively. Next ask yourself how many items you purchased on the last shopping trip that actually weren't needed or that you hadn't intended to purchase when you walked in the door . . . from that shopping trip on, become more aware of what you're doing. Then every time you or your wife reaches for an item of this type—magazines, an expensive brand of toothpaste, paper towels, etc.—stop and put that merchandise back.

One big money fortune builder made a sign which he posted on his shopping cart every time he and his wife went shopping. It said: *"The money you are about to spend can make our fortune."* As a result, they cut these expenditures to practically nothing and added an additional $200 to their big money capital building funds over the next six months.

5) *Unnecessary exorbitant expenses*—patio covers, freezer plans, etc. Generally firms offering items in this manner sell only one type of merchandise and

often utilize both high-powered sales teams and direct telephone solicitation. Frequently the items offered can be bought from a conventional retail outlet for much less.

Ron B. was a $14,000-a-year construction worker. He purchased a food freezer plan for $800. Several months after making this purchase he discovered he could have bought the same freezer from a conventional retail outlet for $400 less. He also estimated that he could have purchased the same quality and quantity of food from a supermarket for $150. Charging fraud, Ron took the matter to court and won. Over the next year he took these savings, combined them with an additional $7000 accumulated over the past two years, and put a down payment on a nearby motel. He then moved his family into the motel manager's apartment rent free, and began to build up the business. Within the next two years he purchased three more motels and several other businesses including an automobile rental agency. At the end of five years he was personally making $70,000 a year, had moved the family to a large country place, and was working hard toward his first million dollars.

Over the years, you'll be deluged with many offers of this type. If you need such merchandise you'd generally be better off to purchase it from a conventional retail outlet. Some of these plans, however, do offer good buys—so before purchasing simply price the same merchandise at several outlets to make sure you never pay more than is absolutely necessary.

POINTS TO REMEMBER

You can free up more fortune-building capital from your present income by selectively changing your lifestyle so you spend less for what you actually need.

Here's how to do it:

1) Pay cash whenever possible.

2) Change your eating habits; utilize smart grocery shopping habits, and cash in on all possible coupon promotions.

3) Bargain for merchandise whenever possible.

4) Barter whenever possible by trading something you don't need for something you want.

4

Plan Backwards
to Millionize
Your Fortune Building

The millionizing of all fortune building basically starts with your budget. In actuality, it tremendously affects when you can start your fortune building activities and how much cash you'll have available when you're ready to start toward your first million. Your budget can be a tremendous fortune-building tool, but your entire attitude toward it is vital. Mentally you can make your budget zoom you along quickly or hold you back unnecessarily. Therefore in making up any budget, each expenditure must take into account the fortune you eventually want to create.

For instance, if you're renting a home for $250 a month and you're a determined fortune builder you'll question whether or not it's possible to get by on $200 so you can put the remainder in your big money capital fund. Or if you've budgeted $250 a month for food, you might question whether it's possible to cut back to $175. This kind of all-consuming desire to build a fortune will make you consider every penny you spend in the light of the big money you eventually intend to make.

If you simply make out a budget and allot so much for food, housing and other everyday items as most people do you will be placing a major obstacle in your own big money path. That way you will be working for your budget—not it for you. You must strive to be completely fortune oriented. Weigh each expenditure you make in the light of whether or not it's possible to pare down the total amount spent so the remainder can be used for big money fortune building.

In addition, try to make even necessary expenses a stepping stone toward your future fortune whenever possible.

James S., for instance, was making $7000 a year as a high school custodian, and owned an extremely small run-down home that his wife kept insisting they remodel. He agreed, but realized that under the crowded conditions of their present home he was going to have a hard time working and needed some place to carry on his fortune-building activities. In doing the remodeling he decided to plan a small office for himself. This gave him a quiet place to work without interference. He then decided to try an automotive mail order business which he launched from his own office.

Within a few years this business expanded into a full time operation grossing over $25,000 a month. At that time James S. moved from his home office into his own building and built his family a much larger home in a fashionable section of town.

There are, of course, many other ways you can utilize your budget as a fortune-building tool, funneling money out of the regular budget for some aspect of fortune building.

Build Your Budget Around Your Fortune Making Activities

Most people attempting to take fortune building capital out of their present income simply decide what their fixed expenses are, then put aside whatever might be left for themselves. Unfortunately, this probably will never get you to your goal.

If you're really serious about fortune building you've got to first decide how much you want to take out that month or year, next establish that as a fixed unmovable budget item, and then work the remainder of the budget around this.

Ray B., for instance, decided to open a small pet shop in a nearby community. Unfortunately, as a $9000-a-year window washer, he had absolutely no capital. The only possibility, Ray realized, was to take the cash out of his own income, acquire some with a part-time job, and then borrow the remainder. Knowing that most people can take 15 percent each month out of their present income, Ray decided to try for 20 percent. He then made out a budget starting with $150 a month for fortune-building capital. Unfortunately, with this item his budget no longer balanced. Undaunted, he cut down the amounts designated for food, clothing and similar items until the budget worked. After that he actually started setting aside the $150 by the pay-yourself-first method described in Chapter 2. Difficult as it was in the beginning, it became easier and easier as the months passed.

At the end of the year Ray took $1800 saved from the yearly budget, $1500 accumulated from a spare time job and $3300 borrowed from a local source, and placed a $6500 down payment on a small neighborhood pet shop.

Continuing to utilize this principle, he saved an additional amount over the next year and at the end of that time opened a similar pet shop in a nearby community. In the same way, he continued to open new outlets whenever possible and eventually wound up with 18 stores. At this point he was making over $40,000 a year in personal income, had a country and city home and five automobiles.

To repeat the rule: Decide exactly how much you want to put aside for fortune building; then work the rest of your budget around it.

Let's see how this works. Say, for instance, you're making $9000 a year and decide to take out 20 percent (that's $180 a month). Make out the remainder of your budget; for example, rent, $200; automobile payment, $85; food, $150; clothing, $30; doctor bills, $15; recreation, $15; gasoline, $30; insurance, $10; telephone, $25; miscellaneous, $38. That's $598—yet you only have $570 left over after subtracting $180 from your take-home pay. When this happens, of course, you must go over your budget and cut back on some of the regular expenditures.

If, for instance, you put off buying clothing, cut the doctor bill back to $10 and gasoline to $27 you can make this particular budget work. Sometimes this means making part payments or no payments at all on particular bills. It is necessary, however, if you expect to reach your big money goals as quickly as possible.

Set Up Big Money Priorities

In establishing a budget that will work for you, you must establish some kind of expense priorities identifying those expenses you can reduce. Simply go over each budget item and ask yourself how important that particular one is to you. For instance, if you really want to live in your present home, put that expense item near the top of the list. If you discover, however, that you don't particularly care what kind of clothing you wear, that expense should go near the bottom of the list. Next ask yourself about food—do you want to continue eating at about the same level or will you accept something less fancy? The same holds true for recreation and all other expenses. Try to discover what's important and what isn't. Those items which wind up at the bottom of your list are the ones that you will now try to cut back. After you've made your decisions then simply go back and really slice into the low priority items. By making these kinds of priority decisions and then acting on them you'll find that your budget cutting becomes almost automatic.

Check Each Budget Item Carefully

Once you have set up your budget so that it is turning out fortune-building capital automatically (and you have established priorities) you must now try to squeeze the last drop of big money potential from it. There is, as we have already seen, lots of waste in most people's present lifestyles. By changing lifestyles selectively and by cutting ruthlessly you can redirect cash to your own big money purposes that would otherwise slip away unnoticed. An example of this is paying $12 for merchandise at one store which you can buy down the street for $10.

At this point go back over your budget carefully and try to reduce each expenditure by 5 percent. You should, of course, reduce the lower priority items even more. Some of these expenditures are fixed, but regardless of that, at least take a look at all of them again. Let's now examine these individual items more closely:

Rent

Generally this is a fixed expense. Sometimes, however, you might want to consider moving into cheaper housing to save money for fortune building. Seattle department store clerk James O., for instance, was paying $250 a month rent for a small house overlooking Lake Union. He decided that while he enjoyed the view, it really wasn't necessary to pay that much in rent.

Jim began to look around and soon discovered a suitable place in a different section of town for $175 a month. He then moved the family into the new place and began putting the additional money in the bank. By the end of the year he had accumulated an extra $400 he could add to his big money capital fund.

Food

As mentioned before there are often hidden expenses in your food budget which are the result of wasteful spending habits and a desire for convenience foods. Go over your food expenditures carefully, referring back to Chapter 3, and try to cut basic food costs by 5 percent.

Clothing

Some clothing purchases are absolutely necessary, but again, by making do and holding off purchases, you can often cut back 5 percent or more here and never know the money is gone.

Insurance

Generally insurance represents a fixed expense, but sometimes by shopping around you can save on automobile insurance and other types. Although life insurance rates are pretty much fixed, you may have more insurance coverage than you need, or you may be able to get adequate coverage by switching to cheaper term insurance. To check on this budget item, call another insurance agent in addition to your own, tell him that you want to reduce your expenditure here, and see what he has to offer. Perhaps it's possible to shift and save additional cash for your big money capital building.

Medical Bills

Some doctor bills are absolutely necessary. Other times people run up medical bills when the need is only marginal.

Sean T., for instance, constantly paid out between $100 and $500 for medical expenses each and every year. Sean had always felt that medical expenses were an absolute fixed necessity, but he decided to give each doctor bill additional scrutiny anyway. What he discovered was that his wife took the children to the doctor any time they made the simplest complaint. The doctor would always give her a prescription and send the kids home. Sean then sat down with his wife and discussed the entire medical problem. In conclusion they decided to make an agreement that unless the children were really sick, she'd try not to panic and take them to the doctor. By the end of the year this had resulted in a savings of about

$150, money Sean could then funnel into more fortune-building capital.

Automobile Payments

Auto payments are also generally a temporary fixed expense that usually can't be lowered. There are a few devices you can use, however, to free up extra cash if necessary. You can sell that particular car and buy a cheaper one, bringing the payments down to a manageable size that will allow you to skim off a little extra. You can also refinance, lowering the present payments and spreading them over a longer time period. This will cost more in the long run but will free capital building money initially. These methods are a little extreme but are usable if you're looking for every last possible cash source.

Loan Payments

To maximize your capital building potential and put yourself in the best possible fortune-building condition, you should get off credit as quickly as possible. In actuality, personal credit is an extreme liability to any serious big money fortune builder because it drains cash without returning any usable asset. If, however, you are now committed to a loan and need to cut payment outgo you can usually refinance to lower present cash payments. This again will cost more over a period of time but will give you the flexibility to produce a capital building surplus right now.

Recreation

Everybody needs recreation and yet it's still possible to cut back by at least 5 percent and not know the difference. Again, set your usual recreational amount, take off 5 percent, and make sure you live up to your commitment.

Miscellaneous

Every budget generally sets aside miscellaneous money to buy tools, fishing tackle, fans, toasters, paper, pencils and other purchases not budgeted elsewhere. Simply set yourself a fixed amount for miscellaneous that's 5 percent or more lower than what you originally planned to spend; then, when you reach that limit, cut yourself off completely.

Stay On Your Budget As If Your Life Depended On It

After you set up your big money capital budget you're going to have to really work to stay within your own limits. What this means is that you have to get tough with yourself and clamp down the minute you find yourself getting out of line. After all, it is your big money future.

A $2000-a-year Cincinnati print shop worker, Oscar H., set up a big money capital building budget to put aside $135 every month. The first month Oscar handled it; the next month he was $25 short, and the third month, $185 short. Under pressure from his creditors he took cash out of his bank account to catch up on back bills. In checking back he realized that several budget items, including food, had exceeded the set limit by $10 to $50. Taking himself in hand, he broke his budget into weekly amounts and insisted that any time he overspent one week, he had to underspend the next. If, for instance, food costs came out too high in one particular week, the family skipped one or two meals the next just to remind themselves to be more careful. After this happened a couple of times, the whole family became exceedingly cost conscious and was soon able to stay on their big money budget almost automatically.

If you find yourself overspending, then, clamp down with some sort of token penalty that will help to make you cost conscious. This can be going without a meal, denying yourself some recreational activity, taking on an extra chore, or almost anything that will drive home the fact that you must stay on your budget.

Remember—this is your big money capital building program. The closer you can stay to your big money budget goals, the faster you'll be able to start your own fortune building.

Imagine Yourself Living It

As a final step, this big money capital building budget must be integrated into your lifestyle so that it becomes habit and second nature. One way to do this is through role playing. After you've set up your new capital building budget, go over the individual items and first imagine what you will have to do to cut costs to that point. Next act it out in your mind. If, for instance, you have decided to cut your food budget from $250 a month to $175, you must first decide what that means, then act out doing whatever is necessary to achieve those goals. In this case, for instance, you might act out having one piece of toast for breakfast every morning, with less butter, one egg instead of two, and so on. This should be continued until you feel comfortable with the new changes. Therefore when you actually start to cut down you'll have much less trouble.

You must also remember here that if you really intend to make significant budget changes, there are usually other family members to consider. What happens, for instance, if you decide on a particular way to spend money and your wife (or husband) won't go along? Naturally in this case your budget probably won't work. The first step, then, is to sit down with the family and talk it over until you reach a general agreement. Then do a little family role playing: talk about what it's going to be like spending in a particular way. See how it feels and try to get each family member to understand exactly what's involved. This way your chances of success will be greatly improved.

Baker B. was a $10,000-a-year factory worker, but had a tremendous desire to begin his own business. Baker had worked up an excellent budget which if followed would produce about $3000 a year. He then put it into effect—but the first month he was only able to take out $74, the second month about $80, and the third $74 again.

He asked himself what had happened and discovered that his wife hadn't agreed with his program and hadn't changed buying habits at all. She continued to shop in the same old ways. For instance, she had just purchased new clothes for the kids, insisted on expensive presents for the children's birthday, picked out expensive convenience foods for dinner and more. All of these were knocking holes in his capital building plan. He then got the family together and talked over exactly what they wanted to do. He also explained how each one could help. At the end of the talk they all agreed that it was a good idea and promised to cut down. They then played a game of acting out what it would be like.

At the end of the next month Baker put aside $280 and was able to stay with the program from then on. Within a year, utilizing all capital building methods, he had enough capital to launch a small contract cleaning business. By the end of the next year the business had ten large accounts grossing $200,000 a year. At this point he gave each family member $1000 to spend as they wanted, bought a new home with a swimming pool in a fashionable section of town, and took them all on an extended vacation so they could really enjoy the reward of their joint budget effort.

POINTS TO REMEMBER

1. You should strive to be completely fortune oriented. Weigh each present budget expenditure carefully to see if it can't be cut down so the remainder can be used for your big money fortune building.

2. Build your budget around your fortune-making activities. Decide how much you want to take out that month or year, establish that as an unmovable budget item, and then work the remainder of the budget around that.

3. Check each budget item carefully and set up big money priorities.

4. Stay on your budget no matter what happens.

5. To make it easier to utilize a big money budget, act it out before you actually try to utilize that particular budget.

5

Moonlight Your Way to a Big Money Nest Egg

In the last few chapters we discussed how to utilize your present income to build a big money nest egg. These methods work wonders in getting you started, but if you're going to launch your real fortune making activities quickly, it's vital that in addition to taking capital from your present income that you supplement this big money accumulation through moonlighting. In other words, you also need to utilize your extra time to boost yourself along to real riches.

Fortunately, every one of us has just as much time available as anyone else. The millionaire doesn't possess any more time for fortune building than you do. The difference is in how that time is used. Most of us spend our leisure in nonproductive activities. We read the newspaper, watch TV, go to the motorcycle races, picnic and much else. These are fine activities but do nothing to further your big money ambitions. Now take a good look at your own schedule. How many hours do you have available between the time you get home and go to bed, and on weekends? Ten hours? Twenty hours? Fifty hours a week or more? If you are really determined, you can turn each and every one of those extra hours into cash. Every year thousands of ambitious fortune makers add to their big money capital pumping gas, selling insurance, clerking part time, and more. This is not done with the idea of adding immediate family income but for the purpose of creating a cash nest egg with which to build a fortune.

Fred C., for instance, is a self-made millionaire whose current business enterprise fund now has total assets of well over $900 million. Fred started a few years ago, with a tremendous determination to create a big money nest egg. He poured concrete driveways in the mornings, pumped gas in the afternoons and sold insurance by night. Within a few years, utilizing this method, he had $10,000 in the bank. Having an interest in stocks, he then took a job as an investment firm trainee, where he specialized in carefully researching firms he felt might have investment potential. When his income from commissions passed the $100,000 mark, he quit and purchased a 20 percent interest in a management company that started to grow immediately. Within a few years this firm's assets reached almost a billion dollars and seemed certain to go even higher. Fred currently advises others on investments, teaches stock market courses at leading universities and generally enjoys life in the upper income bracket.

There are many other examples:

Walt H. decided to build his big money nest egg selling shoes on Saturdays. He simply contacted a company who advertised for direct shoe salesmen in a national magazine. As soon as the samples came he began canvassing the downtown area, calling on local businessmen. At the end of his second month of selling, he started putting aside an additional $300 to $600 a month and wound up the year with a $6000 moon-lighting nest egg. Putting this together with $6000 he had already accumulated from other sources he began a small hot dog stand across the street from a large factory. The stand specialized in 16 kinds of hotdogs, salad and all the coffee you could drink free. This enterprise did so well that he opened ten more stands during the next two years. At the end of this period he sold the entire business for $300,000 and retired temporarily while he got his bearings and decided exactly what to do next.

The well-known case of John Y. Brown illustrates this. To accumulate his nest egg, John Y. Brown sold encyclopedias part time for several years, averaging $16,000 to $25,000 a year. Combining his cash saved with a loan, Brown and Colonel Sanders opened a fast food restaurant, the "Colonel Sanders Porky Pig House." Later Brown convinced Colonel Sanders to let him develop the entire franchise system, which eventually culminated in a $245 million merger.

If you are really serious about developing your own fortune then, you should (like these millionaires) trade your time for money. Let's look at a few of the better ways to moonlight your way to a big money fortune:

Create Fortune-Building Capital With Your Own Services

We are today a service-oriented economy. Years ago people did everything for themselves. Today, however, most people are so busy they don't have the time to handle specialized needs themselves. This provides a tremendous opportunity to add to your big capital nest egg in your spare time, bringing anywhere from $2 to $15 an hour extra. This might include babysitting, house painting, being a part-time handyman, lawn mowing and more.

A Seattle factory worker, George G., decided to try the part-time service route to add to the small amount he'd already set aside. He primarily wanted something that would allow him to work his own hours. George had handled many plumbing chores on his regular job and decided to cash in on a plumbing related service. A lot of people, he noted, were adding sprinkler systems, a specialty of his. He advertised his services in the classified section of the local paper. To do the work he arranged to rent a ditch digger from a local rental firm and bought the needed equipment from a nearby supplier. His charges included the cost of the supplies and the equipment rental plus $10 an hour for himself. Generally he received one to two jobs a week during the season which netted him $200 to $300 a week. At the end of a year and a half George G. discovered he had cashed away a whopping $15,000 big money nest egg. Since he was now making more money part time than from his regular job, he decided to quit the factory job and launch into the sprinkler services full time, utilizing the $15,000 to do so. To do this he simply advertised more, and then added the needed equipment and supplies as the business began to build. Within two years he had 15 employees, $45,000 in basic equipment and a gross income of $350,000 a year.

If the personal service route is for you, ask yourself what you can do to fill other people's needs. Can you type? Babysit? Hang wallpaper? Put in sidewalks? Repair things? Landscape? Next ask if these are services that people in your local area really need. After that, place an ad in the service section of your local newspaper and see what happens.

Now here's a list of services that can be offered in your community. Some of these require a contractor license in some states. Generally, however, you can perform these services as an employee of whoever hires you. Check the license boards in your particular state (their phone numbers are generally found in the telephone yellow pages of your state capital phone book).

Babysitting	Janitorial service
Concrete work	Tree-care service
Hauling	Sewing alterations
Appliance repair	Garden maintenance
Lawn mowing	Spray service
Kitchen remodeling	Bookkeeping
Decorating	Sign painting
Handyman work	Advertising
Painting	House cleaning
Landscaping	Architectural drafting
Paper hanging	Acoustic ceiling work
Typing	Plumbing

Take the Security Path to Riches

Crime has skyrocketed in the past few years, especially in the areas of pilferage, shoplifting and vandalism. While this complicates the security problem tremendously for retail business, schools, factories, government agencies, shopping centers and industrial complexes, it does provide a tremendous opportunity to build your own big money nest egg.

A few years ago few retail firms had their own security forces. Today it is not unusual for a 15-store discount chain, for instance, to employ 15 to 30 people to handle security details. The same is true of schools, colleges and many other institutions. Some now hire their own security forces; others employ private security forces who specialize in this type of work. Security guards sometimes patrol in cars, check doors on foot, handle crowds, and patrol shopping centers as a deterrent. Wages here generally run from $2.00 to $6.00 an hour.

Charles H., who built a $10,000 capital nest egg into a $10-million-a-year automotive parts distributorship, utilized this method to accumulate capital.

While working on a low-paying fence building crew for a local contractor, Charles decided that he could easily spend an additional four to five hours every day as a security guard. The job Charles obtained was to check buildings for five hours a day with another officer.

At the end of the year he borrowed $2500, and put it together with $2500 moonlighting money and $2500 taken from income. With this he opened a small parts discount store in a low-rent section of town. This proved so popular that he opened five stores within the next year, and then a parts warehouse which distributes discount auto parts throughout the state. At this point his take-home income topped $80,000 a year and was still going up.

If this type of moonlighting interests you, you can approach it several ways: (1) For retail department store-discount store-factory security jobs, call the company's personnel office to ask them if they have a security force and how you go about applying. Some stores don't hire people part time, but many do. (2) Private security forces often advertise in the classified help wanted sections of your local paper. Simply check these regularly and call the ones that appeal to you.

A few years ago security jobs were difficult to obtain; today, however, this is an almost surefire guaranteed big money income that you can cash in on at almost a moment's notice.

Try the Part-Time Firm Route to a Big Money Nest Egg

While many firms do not hire part-time help directly they do hire temporary help from firms who specialize in providing this type of service. There are a number of firms throughout the United States: Manpower Inc., Kelly Services, Western Girl Inc. and others which specialize in providing a wide variety of people for many needs: inventory taking, interviewing, telephone soliciting, passing out samples, engineering help, drafting, secretarial help and more.

George H., for instance, was an $8000-a-year school teacher who was attempting to accumulate enough cash to start a rental equipment business, decided he could add big cash to his income by moonlighting for local business firms. He tried several without luck, then called one of the temporary help firms and asked if they handled this type of job. From then on George worked part time Saturdays and some evenings. The result: a $2000 moonlighting nest egg accumulated by the end of the year. Adding $10,000 from other sources, he opened for business the following spring in a new residential section of town. This proved so successful that he expanded five times the first year, added a complete line of recreational equipment the second, and within four years was grossing well over $300,000 a year.

To explore this route, check under temporary help firms (or employment—temporary) in the Yellow Pages. Simply call them and ask what positions they have available.

Part-Time Sales Create Big Money Potential

If you're sales oriented, this may be for you. While regular salespersons often are paid relatively small amounts of money on a regular hourly basis, some part-time sales jobs deal only with big money merchandise: mobile homes, recreational vehicles, swimming pools, mountain cabins and similar items. Generally these companies pay on a commission basis and will often allow you to work evenings and weekends. Just one sale of a large ticket item per week can yield $700 to $1000.

Ron G., for instance, was interested in creating a big money nest egg fast. He felt he could make it in a hurry if he could get a part-time job with a large and aggressive recreational vehicle dealer. He initially called, talked to the dealer about his interest in part-time selling, and then went in for an interview. The dealer gave Ron two days training and put him to work evenings and Saturdays. In the first three weeks Ron failed to make one sale. After that, however, things started to pop. At the end of the year Ron had accumulated well over $11,000 in commissions, sometimes selling three to eight recreational vehicles a week.

If this kind of selling appeals to you, simply decide what's being sold in your area that pays big money commissions: Mobile homes? Swimming pools? Package homes? Summer cabins? Generally you find these firms in the telephone yellow pages. Just look through and see what's being sold that costs $1000 or more each. Then call, set up an appointment, and go talk to them. Many will be glad to give you a try on a part time basis . . . the rest is up to you.

Part-Time Retail Help—Your Path To Riches

If you have some craft or building speciality you may well want to consider the possibility of putting this to use part time.

Now that the do-it-yourself field has become big, many retail firms specializing in selling to the do-it-yourself market like to employ part-time people who have some trade skill: plumbers, carpenters, electricians and others—or someone who has specialized in a craft like leather work.

One firm—Handyman Inc. of La Mesa, California, with a number of retail stores—makes it a practice to hire part-time people to work in their specialities. People who know what they're doing, the firm finds, make the best kind of sales help since they are able to offer expert advice to the inexperienced do-it-yourselfer. Today many firms in the home improvement field offer this kind of job, including modern retail lumber yards and home improvement stores with do-it-yourself departments. You will find these firms listed under "Building Materials" in the Yellow Pages. Again, simply call and ask for an appointment. In addition, many department, discount and specialty stores add part-time help at peak times; again, you will find these listed in the Yellow Pages.

Besides the particular areas discussed here you will find moonlighting jobs available in many other areas: services stations, restaurants, neighborhood shops and more. Generally, however, the ones discussed here currently offer the best opportunity to start fast and quickly pile up a good-sized big money nest egg. Whatever you do, however, moonlighting is almost an absolute must if you expect to multiply your nest egg quickly to the point where you're ready to begin your big money fortune making.

POINTS TO REMEMBER

Moonlighting is a vital part of your big capital accumulation. Here are some sources you should try:

Pyramid sales jobs: These offer direct sales commissions and a chance to make additional profit as a distributor.

Service businesses: Services, babysitting, painting, garden maintenance and others offer tremendous potential today.

Part-Time Security Jobs: Due to the increase in all types of crime, part-time security job openings are now on the increase.

Part-Time Firms: Part-time firms often offer a chance for additional cash taking inventory, canvassing by phone, etc.

Part-Time Sales: More and more retail firms are now putting on part-time help for peak hours. Building materials firms also like to employ skilled people to help their do-it-yourself customers.

6

How to Borrow Your Way to Great Wealth

Big money fortune building nearly always needs at least some borrowed money to get it off to a really good start. Borrowing is one of the vital cogs in reaching your capital building goal. Start by taking as much cash as you can from your present income. Add to it by picking up extra cash wherever you can, and when you get within striking distance of your big money goal, use borrowed money to make it an instant reality. How much you can borrow will depend on how much cash you already have and on several other factors we'll take up shortly. Sometimes, however, you'll be able to borrow more than you ever dreamed possible.

Ray H., for instance, was an $8000-a-year cook in a nationally franchised fast food house. Ray grew sick and tired of always being in debt. Working in the fast food business every day Ray saw giant fortunes being made there by the average guy without any more talent or education than he had, and decided he'd like to try the business for himself.

Over the next year and a half Ray faithfully took $150 a month from his income and added an extra $100 a month by working overtime at a local service station.

During this capital building period he carefully studied the restaurant chain he was working for, trying to determine their strong points and weaknesses. After a year Ray prepared a prospectus stating that he wanted to open a hot sandwich shop. He outlined the entire method of operation, including portion control, accounting and advertising, in great detail.

As soon as he managed to put together $4500 in capital he began making the rounds of local banks with his prospectus. When several turned him down he stopped trying banks and began looking for other kinds of backers with extra cash. Within a few weeks his complete prospectus so impressed a local car dealer that the dealer immediately decided to put up $50,000 to start the operation—more than Ray had ever hoped for in the beginning.

Instead of renting a building, Ray and his sponsor decided to buy a lot on a traveled highway and build to their own specifications. Ray supervised the entire construction and wasn't satisfied until each detail had been completed to his liking.

Ray's restaurant was an instant success; over 2000 customers lined up outside on opening morning to take advantage of his initial 1¢ sandwich special. From then on there was no stopping the growth. By the end of the year Ray and his backer opened five more outlets. At this point Ray was taking home $700 a week with the prospect of more to come. He also bought his wife and two grown children each a car, moved the family to a swanky section of town and began looking for a second home at the seashore.

When starting your capital building planning, you initially will want to include all three methods of accumulating a big money nest egg. In the beginning, just divide the amount you want into thirds; that's what you will expect to put together from each method. Generally that's a good estimate of what you can borrow, since most lenders are conservative. But with persistance, good planning and a little luck, it's possible to come up with many times that amount.

How To Know When To Stop Saving and Ask
Others For Cash

Up to this point in this book we've stressed accumulating big money capital. In many cases the only way you're going to get a chance to strike out toward your own giant fortune is to accumulate the necessary capital yourself. That's why we've discussed this in such detail.

It's equally important, however, to know when to stop saving and to ask others for cash. Why? Building a big money nest egg yourself is slow money accumulation, while doubling the value of that nest egg within a short time in your own business is fast money accumulation. To make really big money you must stop accumulating slow money as soon as possible and turn to methods that multiply your money making efficiency.

Sanderson B., for instance, was a $9000-a-year warehouse worker with hospital debts to pay off. He wanted to open a small donut shop and coffee house in one of San Francisco's outlying districts, and he could successfully begin business with $5000. He then began to accumulate the necessary cash. By the end of the first year, utilizing present income methods and moonlighting, Sanderson B. had put aside $1900. At this point, instead of trying to put the rest aside himself, he talked each of 50 coworkers into putting up $60 each. With this money he then opened the business and started letting customers help him accumulate fast cash. So successful was his idea that by the end of six months he had taken in almost $3000 over and above basic costs. While at this point Sanderson hadn't paid back any of his investors, he had accumulated an additional $3000 in half the time it had taken to put together his original $1900. This is a good example of why you should stop accumulating slow money as quickly as possible and start doing it the fast way.

Now let's look at a method that will let you know when to stop saving and start borrowing. Every business is different and the amount you can borrow will depend on how risky your business venture is, how much money you have to put up, how well you've planned, how good a presentation you have put together and how much confidence you instill in other people. To make an intelligent decision now, rate yourself on the following Loan Risk Rating Chart.

Loan Risk Rating Chart

Question	Rating 1-2-3-4-5

1. How speculative is the business I plan to start?

   If you intend to buy a well-established money making business, rate this 5. If you intend to prospect for oil, rate it 0. Estimate between these two where you think your proposed business might rate.

2. How much money have you accumulated?

   If you have most of the money you need but must borrow a few hundred more, rate this 5. If you have to borrow about what you'll accumulate, rate it 3. If you expect to borrow all but a few hundred, rate it 1.

3. How well have you planned what you intend to do? Have you put together a good presentation?

   Prospective lenders (no matter who they are) want to be confident that you know what you're doing. You must take the time to think out all details. If you have thought the project out in complete detail and have made up a good written presentation, give yourself 5. If you have a a good idea but haven't made up a written presentation, give yourself 3. If you haven't thought either out clearly, give yourself 0.

4. How much confidence do other people have in you?

Some people naturally instill confidence in others and people will trust them with their last dollar. Others don't instill confidence at all. Ask yourself if people seem to trust you instinctively. If so, rate yourself 5. Do you have a hard time gaining confidence and trust? If so, rate yourself 0. If you fall in between, then rate yourself somewhere on the scale between 1 and 5.

When finished, add up the totals. If you rate above 15, and have accumulated at least $500, stop saving and go looking for additional money. You may not be able to borrow at first, but if you're really determined to turn slow money into fast money as quickly as possible keep at it until you actually get the cash. In this way you'll often cut months or years off the time required to build your big money fortune.

Milton R., for instance, a $9000-a-year Chicago retail store employee, began putting aside $200 a month with the idea of raising $15,000. Milton's goal was to launch a small automotive parts discount house, and he had carefully researched the idea, put together many statistics gathered from banks and government agencies, decided on a location and prepared a written statement of what he wanted to do. When Milton had accumulated $1000, he rated himself 19 on the loan risk chart and decided to give it a whirl. Several bankers turned him down, but a local businessman with money to invest became intrigued because of the current do-it-yourself auto repair craze and decided to back Milton. They rented a store in a lower-middle income neighborhood, stocked the building and started to advertise. The idea caught on well, since more and more people were forced to handle their own auto repairs. Within six months, the store started taking in over $10,000 a month and began to build additional cash fast.

By asking for a loan before he thought he was completely ready, Milton got started rapidly and was able to cut months off the time it would normally have required to launch a fortune-building business.

Make Sure You Really Have Something to Offer

Naturally if you expect someone to loan you money on a fortune-building project it has to be feasible—after all, anyone who intends to loan money wants some assurance they're going to get the money back along with a good profit. Before you start prospecting for loan money, therefore, make sure your project is sound. This three-point check list should help you decide:

1. Does what you have in mind appear to be a good business? Don't make this a technical question. Just use common sense and look for the obvious good points or problems. If you intend to open a restaurant with reasonable prices in a fairly good neighborhood, it probably has a reasonable chance. But if you intend to open an ice cream parlor in a ritzy neighborhood and run it mornings only, its chances are probably poor. Rate what you intend to do as we did before on the 0 to 5 scale.

2. Does your proposed fortune-building business fit your talents? Again, just generally try to decide if your new business fits the talents you already have. Perhaps, for instance, you want to start a small mail order firm which requires you to manage two or three people, advertise, and put a product in the mail. If, you haven't done anything like this, up to this point, you must now make sure that you can handle these tasks. Don't get technical; just make a good guess.

   Henry B., for instance, a Los Angeles bus driver who was tired of living on an inadequate paycheck, decided to start a tennis school with himself as the first instructor. Later he planned to hire others. Since Henry had already given lessons at a local high school evenings, he knew he could handle the instruction, and because he had taken a course in bookkeeping he felt qualified to take care of the paperwork. He also had the ability to handle people well and reasoned there wasn't anything else in this particular business that would prove to be a stumbling block.

George R., on the other hand, wanted to open a snowmobile dealership. George, a Denver telephone company worker, was good at repairing mechanical equipment, but he found he couldn't sell well since he was shy and could hardly talk to people. He went ahead anyway, but unfortunately his sales ability proved a tremendous handicap and he made only two sales during the first five months. If George had stopped to consider his sales deficiencies in the first place instead of simply deciding the business would work out because he loved snowmobiles, he would have anticipated the problems. As it was, the business quickly went under and George wound up working for the telephone company again.

In deciding whether you match the fortune-making business you have in mind, simply sit down and sketch out in a general way what you'll have to do. Then go over each part and ask yourself if you can perform that particular task without difficulty. When you're through, sum it all up in your mind and give yourself a 0 to 5 rating. If you already have the training or talent for most tasks, rate yourself 5. If you already have the training or talent for only a few of the necessary tasks, rate yourself 0. Simply estimate your rating between these.

3. Can you begin your proposed fortune-building business for the amount of capital you can easily obtain? There's nothing more disheartening than starting with too little money, since it always seems like you're working against tremendous odds.

If, for instance, you tried to go into the recreational vehicle business (where many units cost over $5000) with $5000, you'd be asking for a lot of headaches because you'd use up all your money buying one or two units and would have nothing left for lot rental or other business expenses.

But if you took that $5000 and began a bike rental business you might well expect to succeed, since your $5000 would go a long way. In deciding, ask yourself practically how much you think you might need; also, talk to people in similar businesses, keeping in mind what they've had to invest. Then compare what's needed with the amount you think you can raise.

After that, if you think you can easily obtain the needed capital, rate your proposed business 5. If it seems almost impossible in a reasonable amount of time, rate it 0. Now add the three ratings together. If the total rating adds up to 9 or more then go ahead and try for the needed big money loan. If it is less, you should rethink your proposed fortune-making activity.

Anticipate All Questions To Attract Big Money.

Anyone who loans money wants to be convinced they are putting their money in a good sound investment. Ordinarily these people will insist on having a concrete idea of any business proposition. Many institutions utilize special forms for this. With informal backers you can often simply sit down and talk to them face to face. When you intend to ask for money, however, it always pays to make the best presentation possible. It also pays to anticipate all questions a potential backer might ask and then answer them yourself. This will give the impression that you've done your homework well.

Harry V. was a low-paid Los Angeles school employee, tired of owning only one suit and never having any extra cash.

Harry started his own company to produce a new improved school desk top. After accumulating $3500 he approached several banks and other loan sources that turned him down. At this point Harry began to wonder if his presentation was convincing enough. Deciding that this was his problem, he asked his wife to listen to what he had to say and ask as many questions as she could think of. They kept at it until his presentation was letter perfect. As a result, he gave an excellent presentation the next time and fielded every question without difficulty. When Harry finished, the potential backer whipped out his checkbook and wrote a check for every penny asked. The idea was so successful (a recreational vehicle accessory discount supermarket) that it took off like a rocket. Harry sold the company eight months later and pocketed a cool $400,000 with which to continue fortune building along another line.

Put It In Writing To Millionize Your Chances

Learning to field all questions and make the best presentation possible is vital to your success at finding money. So is putting your proposal in writing. Somehow a written proposal is much more convincing to a potential lender than any other method. Jenny W. found that out. She was a low-paid Memphis retail clerk who wanted to set up a small fabric shop in a nearby community. Jenny had at this point managed to set aside $5000, but figured she needed about $10,000 additional for inventory, rent and other basic expenses. She first tried the local bank without any luck; then she started looking for other backers. Unfortunately, however, no one seemed willing to put up the money. Finally Jenny decided to make her proposal clearer. She then sat down wrote out the proposal as carefully as possible, had it printed for $15 and packaged it in an attractive cover.

In the proposal Jenny carefully outlined her business proposition, detailed the profit potential and explained exactly how she intended to invest every dollar. She then took pictures of several shops she liked and included possible layouts and fixtures in the written presentation. Within a week she had all the money she needed with a promise of much more as soon as the profits started to roll in.

The rule, then, is to give yourself the best possible chance of obtaining borrowed money by putting your ideas in writing. You need to:

1. State your proposal clearly. Detail it as much as possible. For instance, if you intend to start a restaurant, describe what you want to do, the type of facilities you intend to have, the size of the dining room, the type of furnishings, the decor and any other pertinent information.

   Try always to include a unique angle. This can be a different way of handling the public, or an unusual way of merchandising the product, pricing, packaging or anything else that makes your business unique. Business success today often depends on doing something more quickly or more efficiently, or in catching the public fancy in an unusual and a different way.

   In a restaurant, for example, you might have an unusual way of setting up the kitchen (for instance, the installation of an oven which allows you to cook the entire meal in seven or eight minutes). You might run a telephone restaurant and have printed menus mailed to everyone within your trading area. The customer makes the selection, calls, allows five minutes, and then drives in to the pickup window. Your unique idea might be a cave decor with all waiters and waitresses in caveman dress. Spell out all angles in complete detail.

2. Include possible costs. Research this as carefully as possible. Try to estimate going-into-business expenses. If you're starting a retail business, for instance, estimate rental costs, remodeling expenses, equipment, supply, inventory costs and all others.

Simply sit down and make a list of everything you might need. Look up firms selling these goods or services in the Yellow Pages, call and get prices. Be as accurate and complete as possible.

3. Estimate possible revenues and operating expenses. This is difficult. Start by surveying similar businesses, talk to the owner and ask for generalized costs and revenues. Most people are eager to help beginners. In addition, the Small Business Administration offers profiles of many businesses—paint stores, bicycle shops and similar retail operations—which will give you some idea of the capital needed plus other useful information. Simply look up the address of the nearest office in the phone book (these are listed in most large city phone books); then write and ask about the particular business in which you're interested.

4. Utilize pictures whenever possible. Look for businesses similar to yours and take pictures of each step of the operation. A small polaroid picture will do. Make sure you photograph any detail that would be useful in carrying out your unique idea or angle. Pictures are always useful in convincing prospective lenders that you have done your homework well.

5. Package your proposal attractively. There are a couple of ways to do this. Have it typed up then package in a attractive folder (buy these at any office supply store). Have the proposal printed by a quick print shop and add stiff covers (about $30). Most printers can package this for you in several ways. This may seem like window dressing, but as one well known super salesman explains, "you can always sell the sizzle a lot easier than you can sell the steak." This principle is a universal

selling truth and should be utilized whenever possible.

How To Convince Your Banker That You Have Big Money Potential

Bankers are sometimes an excellent source of big money capital; once in awhile they'll loan you a great deal more than you think possible. In the past, many present-day millionaires have started on their way to a giant fortune through the bank method.

Don T., a well-known mobile home millionaire, began his drive toward a big money fortune working in a cabinet shop at $1.18 an hour. After a stint in a mobile home factory, he and nine others founded a new mobile home company. At that point Don T. had saved $2000 in fortune-building capital; he borrowed the rest from the bank. From this point on the firm prospered and when Don sold out in 1969 he received a check for $2,667,000 for his share of the business. The well known real estate man, Bill Mau, also took the bank path to a giant fortune. Utilizing his savings and a conventional bank loan, Mau opened a hamburger stand on Waikiki's Kuhio Beach. At this point he kept his job and ran the hamburger stand at night. During the next several years Mau increased his original equity of $10,000 to $100,000. From there Mau begin to dabble in real estate, buying Hawaiian land. Today Bill Mau's personal wealth is estimated at $13 million dollars plus an annual income of well over $500,000.

Bankers, however, are extremely conservative. They generally dislike making loans to new businesses and often refuse to loan to anyone without extensive business experience.

There are ways, however, that smart money capital builders can get around these built-in bank drawbacks and obtain all the money needed at favorable rates. This is called banker preconditioning. The trick is to convince the banker ahead of time that you are reliable and have a sound business proposition that a banker can safely invest in. Here's how it's done:

Step 1. Start a savings account in one particular bank. As you begin to accumulate capital put it all in this one account.

Step 2. Borrow a small amount and pay it back fast. After you have accumulated a fairly good amount in your bank account, go to that bank and borrow a small amount—$250 to $500. Don't use it, but turn around and pay it back fairly rapidly. This will cost you some interest but it's part of your plan for instilling bank confidence in your ability to pay.

Step 3. Go to one of the bank officers, preferably the manager; tell him you're planning to start a business. Explain the details and ask him how he thinks you should proceed. This makes him partly responsible. If you then seem to follow his advice in the future he will feel obligated to help you along.

Step 4. Take out an additional loan, a little larger this time (between $500 to $1000). Again, pay it back fairly rapidly. This should be done about six months before you intend to launch your fortune-building business.

Step 5. Now you can actually apply for the loan you need. By this time the bank knows you have money on deposit and that you have a good paying record. In addition, the manager is familiar with and partially responsible for your proposed business. When you are given an application to fill out, however, do it carefully. Remember that the bank looks for stability.

There are four major items to watch for on any loan application: length of residence, length of employment or time in business, credit references, and total assets.

Length of residence: To a potential creditor, few moves and long residency in one location mean stability. Always put your best foot forward. If you have lived in one house eight years, then a couple of places five to six months and the last one five years, drop the short residences and put down five years current residence and eight years past residence.

Length of employment or time in business: As with residence, if you have changed employment frequently you should list only the last and the longest one. Creditors generally feel that the longer you've been on a particular job and the fewer moves, the better you'll pay off your loan—so within reason, show the greatest possible stability.

Credit references: You can make yourself appear a better loan risk by carefully screening the reference you list on your application. A credit granter looks at the quality of your references as well as the total number. Do list banks, good department stores, all national credit cards. Don't list retail credit jewelers, loan companies, discount stores and similar businesses. The latter grant credit more easily than the former and are one of the signs some credit grantors look at when trying to determine the quality of the loan they are about to make.

Total assets: Loan officers like to look at your total assets (the total value of everything you own). Put down every last possible asset. Your car, furniture, bonds, savings accounts, houses, boats and all miscellaneous items. Always overestimate their worth. If you think your house is worth about $25,000, put down $28,000 to $30,000. If your car is worth $1000, put down $1300. The idea is to exaggerate slightly so your net worth comes out as high as possible.

Banks also lend money in several ways. The most popular from the banks viewpoint is the discount loan. For instance if you borrow $1000 for one year at ten percent, the bank will deduct $100 and credit your account with $900. You never had the use of the entire $1000 and are paying an effective rate of 20 percent a year. Accept this kind of loan only at a last resort.

The cheapest way to borrow is the straight business loan. Here you borrow the entire sum to be repaid. A $1000 loan for one year at ten percent, for instance, will be repaid in full with 1100 at the end of the 12-month period. The entire $1000 here is deposited in your account. Whenever possible, insist on this type of loan.

How To Mine Other Traditional Loan Sources

Besides banks there are other traditional loan sources that you should be able to use successfully. Let's look at them.

1. *Home Mortgage Refinancing*

We mentioned this briefly in Chapter 2. If you purchased your home some years ago it undoubtedly has gone up considerably; this increase may well be more than enough to start you on your fortune-building path.

Cranston T., for instance, found an unexpected source of financing. Cranston was a $700-a-month Boston fast food worker who wanted to start his own restaurant. He bought a small home years before on a GI loan and promptly forgot about its big money potential. When it came time to borrow fortune-building money, however, one of Cranston's friends mentioned that he might tap a gold mine by refinancing his home rather than trying for a straight loan. Much to his surprise, with the accumulated principle and value increase, Cranston found he now had an $18,000 nest egg he could use.

With his $2000 savings and the $18,000 from his house Cranston then rented a building, decorated it and conducted an extensive advertising campaign offering free hamburgers. On opening day crowds thronged in and continued to bring him repeat business for several months afterwards. Cranston wound up the year with a $10,000 profit, the second with $30,000. Soon after that he moved into an exclusive section of town, sent his children to expensive private schools and bought himself a new houseboat for an extensive five-month vacation.

To obtain this financing, simply go to banks and savings and loan associations, tell them what you want to do, and see what they have to offer.

2. *Finance Companies*

If you can't borrow from a bank or similar source, it's usually possible to borrow $1000 to $5000 from a finance company. Simply go to them with your proposition. They will often insist on a second mortgage on your house in return for the money. They also charge fairly high interest.

3. *Credit Unions*

You must be a credit union member to borrow from this source. But in many cases you can join at work or buy a membership from a non-work related credit union for from $10 to $20. Some credit unions are so loosely formed that you can easily qualify. The Church Council Credit Union, for instance, is open to all church members. Simply look them up under credit unions in the Yellow Pages, call and find out what their membership qualifications are. Once you join you can ask for money in the conventional manner (usually $300 to $5000).

4. *Money By Mail*

It's possible today to borrow money by just writing for it. Banks are better, but if other methods fail you can try this one. You'll find several hundred firms specializing in money by mail and most will loan anywhere from $150 to $1500. To find them, buy current copies of *Popular Science, Mechanix Illustrated, Science and Mechanics* and similar magazines, and write for the firms' literature. Rates are high, so compare carefully before borrowing.

5. *The Small Business Administration*

The Small Business Administration generally doesn't loan for new business but there are some exceptions (such as loans for minority businesses). It's also a good type of loan to keep in mind later on when you need money for fortune-building business expansion.

There are three types of loans available: the direct loan (when you've tried to obtain financing from banks or other institutions without luck), the guarantee loan (where the SBA guarantees up to 90 percent of the amount borrowed, and the participation loan (banks or other lending institutions furnish 25 percent; the SBA furnishes the rest). You can find the nearest SBA office listed in the phone books of most large cities.

6. *How To Find Backers Who Will Loan You Money*

Many present-day millionaires feel the best place to obtain big money for fortune-building is from well-off backers who have extra money to invest and are looking for an enterprise with real big money potential.

Wendell C., for instance, made a fortune in nursing homes. Wendell didn't have nearly enough capital when he was ready to build his first nursing home, so he convinced a contractor, a building supply proprietor, an architect and two real estate men, to each put up $1000 and contribute his services or profit for an equity in the nursing home. This first investment paid off so handsomely that they decided to start others. Today Wendell C. serves as chairman of the board of several Kentucky corporations and has over $5 million in the bank.

Saul S., whose company now generates annual revenues in excess of $650 million a year, was turned down by Chase Manhattan Bank, but after restructuring his proposed company in a way that would provide tax shelter for wealthy individuals, he rounded up a group of investors who were willing to put up money.

I mentioned John Y. Brown earlier. He was the fortune builder who bought out Colonel Sanders of Kentucky Fried Chicken. Brown convinced a backer who had already made a fortune in surgical supplies to put up the money for this venture. Brown went on from there to accumulate a personal fortune in excess of $31,000,000.

Generally you have two ways: you can take in a number of small backers for a percentage of your profit, or you can find one backer willing to put up the entire amount.

When looking for small backers, start with friends, then go to people who might be involved with the type of business you intend to launch. If, for instance, you intend to build apartments, try real estate people, architects, building supply owners and the like. Simply make up a written proposal, call and make an appointment, and then outline your proposal in person. You will sometimes get turned down, but keep at it until you find enough backers to put you over the top. There's a truism which says that if you're convinced that what you want to do is right, then you'll always attract more cash than you know what to do with.

To find single backers, start with people who own fairly large businesses in your community—car dealers, department store owners, large contractors, trucking firm owners. Make up a list of possibilities from your own knowledge. Call and make appointments; then go in person. Frequently these people are looking for good investments and have been known to put up anything from $1,000 to over $1,000,000 just on the basis of an idea. In addition, watch for retired business owners in your community. If the owner of a successful business has retired and sold out, he is probably looking for a way to make money with his extra cash. Contact these people the same way you would any single backer.

POINTS TO REMEMBER

Stop saving and start asking others for cash as quickly as possible.

It is important to start accumulating money the fast way in business instead of by the slower savings or moonlighting methods. Borrowing allows you to jump quickly from one type of money accumulation to the other.

Gauge when to start asking for money by rating yourself on the loan risk rating chart (p. 88).

Make sure you have a business that someone would loan money to by checking your proposed fortune-building business with the three point check list (p. 90).

To attract big loan money, anticipate all possible business questions and put your proposal in writing.

Consider the following sources of fortune-building capital:

Banks
Home mortgage financing
Credit unions
Money by mail
The Small Business Administration
Backers who will put up money

Banks sometimes loan money to business newcomers if you establish a track record with that particular bank, make yourself known to the bank officers and get them in on your potential big money business right from the beginning.

Successful businessmen and retirees often have extra cash to invest. Many present-day millionaires have utilized this path to giant riches.

7

How To "Fortune-Build" With Created Capital (How To Start a Fortune-Making Business)

Creating a big money fortune should be easy and almost automatic from beginning to end—but initially it's up to you to set up the conditions that will make you a big money winner. You must make definite, positive decisions about your fortune goals. Napoleon Hill, in his book *Think and Grow Rich* (Fawcett Publications, Inc.), insists that you write down exactly how much money you want and generally indicate how you intend to go about accumulating that kind of cash. Go over and over your plan mentally, then, until it is deeply ingrained in your subconscious and the money itself has become a burning desire.

That's exactly what you should do here. Get yourself a notebook—a small one will do—and before you even start to accumulate capital, write down in general terms what kind of a fortune you want (in dollars and cents) and generally how you intend to create it.

If you have some idea that you want to make big money building apartments, write down *"real estate, apartments."* If you think that you'll enter the restaurant business, put that down. You don't have to go into elaborate detail, but the more definite you become, the more easily you can bring your fortune into actuality later on.

Along with these written plans, give yourself proposed times in which you intend to actualize your big money plans. For instance, write down: "I will accumulate $3000 from present income and $1500 from moonlighting by May 1, (whatever year); I will borrow an additional $6000 by July 1. I will then start preparing my business by July 15, launch it August 28 and be taking in $10,000 a month by the next April."

These times needn't be rigid, but they will make you work to reach your target date. The more concrete and real you can make this in your own mind, the more likely you are to reach your big money goals near the dates you have set.

James D., decided to change his luck and to put life on his side. James, a $9000 a year Chicago factory worker had just managed to make ends meet most of his life and had seen one daughter crippled because he didn't have enough money to pay for expensive hospital treatment.

He sat down one night and made out a fortune guide schedule which stated: "Put aside $4500 by July 1 of next year. Borrow an additional $6000 by August 1. Open an appliance repair business September 1 and take in $50,000 by January 1 of the following year."

James experienced some difficulty in beginning his savings program and didn't manage to accumulate the $4500 until December 15. He also experienced difficulty in borrowing $6000 until the following March when he found a silent partner willing to put up the money. By July 15 he opened for business in a small downtown location. Business came in slowly until he started to advertise; then things picked up considerably. By September 15 he had grossed $12,000; by December 1, $25,000 and by the following July, $65,000. James, of course, missed his target date, but definite time goals and big money intensity kept him working until the paper goals became reality.

To be realistic with your own big money time goals, however, you should adjust your target dates as you go along so if you miss one you still have a good possibility of meeting the rest.

Start Small—Grow Big Fast

Believe it or not, there's a trick to this big money fortune-building business that will make any project multiply faster than you ever dreamed possible. That trick is simply to start small and grow big fast. Too simple? Not really.

To change slow money accumulation into fast money accumulation you must launch your fortune-making business at the first possible moment. We've already talked about this. In addition, however, no matter how much capital you have available you should start fairly small, then use some of that capital for very rapid expansion.

If you're going into a retail business, for instance, begin with the smallest possible space in which you can do business. This saves money initially on rent, inventory and other expenses. If you are purchasing houses for rental or something similar, the same rule applies. It also allows any expansion to create a tremendous impact. Once in business you must expand rapidly to create the kind of movement that will zoom you on to a giant fortune. No matter what kind of business you decide to enter, the same rule applies.

Ben R. a former Seattle insurance company employee who retired on a $6000 a year pension, decided to open a small bookstore in a nearby community. Ben had at that point accumulated about $22,000 in fortune-making capital that he had saved over a lifetime of extremely hard work. Instead of utilizing all of this capital initially, he rented a small 20-foot by 20-foot store in the downtown area and purchased about $3500 worth of books as stock. He spent the first six months letting the community come to know him and building up his stock of books gradually until he had invested about $7000. At this point, Ben suddenly rented a large 1800-square-foot store across from the town's busiest shopping center and moved in, again adding additional inventory. He still only utilized half the available space, however, dropping in a moveable partition to keep the space manageable. At about one-month intervals he moved the wall back an additional ten feet and added another $500 to $1000 worth of books. This periodic expansion gave the impression that things were happening fast at Ben's bookstore. Customers began to tell other people about how well he was doing and business started to pick up. At the end of the first year and a half Ben was grossing almost $1500 a month—unheard of in the book business—made possible because people believed that Ben's business was skyrocketing and wanted to be in on some of the action. At the end of two years, Ben opened three more stores nearby, which simply confirmed the fact that Ben was an active businessman.

At this point he was raking in over $10,000 a month in personal income, had a huge home on a bluff overlooking a nearby river and was negotiating to buy a 1000-acre ranch in Nevada.

Rapid expansion, then, creates its own movement. The store that is doing big business and shows it, always draws additional trade because people like to do business where other people are doing business. The rule, then is: start wherever you are, but expand rapidly the first six months to a year to create the impression that you are really going places fast!

Look For Ideas With Fortune-Building Potential

Some businesses do quite well, but never really create a sensational success. The corner drugstore, for instance, does an adequate business and makes money, but never really pays off big. There are others—answering services, florist shops, cleaners and more—that are all good solid businesses that make money but never seem to contain that extra spark that can unexpectedly create a huge fortune almost overnight.

Some businesses, however, are tuned so well to the times that they simply take off. You might say that the time for that basic idea has come. Over the past few years this has happened to water beds, speed and custom high performance auto parts, and some areas of the fast food business, for example. It was possible in each of these areas to start on a shoestring and strike it rich within a few short years.

Ted McE., for instance, when he entered business a number of years ago, had an idea that the demand for high performance (hot-rod) auto parts by teenagers would skyrocket. Volume had up to this point been fairly small. Ted, however, borrowed $300 from a local bank, talked a number of manufacturers into shipping him merchandise on consignment and put $300 down on a small store in a run-down section of town. Fortunately Ted anticipated the trend correctly for the fad to "hot-rod" cars had just begun to catch on. In the first month the kids almost bought out his entire stock. The same thing happened the second month. After that Ted McE. gradually began to enlarge his inventory. By the end of the year he had grossed just a little over $100,000. The next year business zoomed to $300,000 and after that there was no stopping the growth. Within six years Ted had opened seven new stores with a net worth of over eight million dollars. He realized at that point that demand had started to decline so he accepted a lucrative six million dollar offer and moved on into another business.

Leisure-related businesses are another basic idea area that offer tremendous potential. Bob F. of Portland, Oregon reasoned that people needed leisure-related activities and also like to be involved in whatever they were doing. The outgrowth of this was an old-fashioned ice cream parlor with a new twist: all patron birthdays were announced with the beating of a drum. For special ice cream orders a siren wailed and to the beating of a base drum four waiters ran up and down the aisles carrying the ice cream dish.

This generated tremendous excitement and involved everyone in the place. In addition, Bob instructed all personnel to be extremely friendly and smile a lot. Although he felt originally that the concept would appeal mainly to children, he soon discovered that adult customers were hungry for "involvement" and flocked to the parlor in droves. Within a short time Bob opened several additional parlors and started a franchise chain that spread up and down the West Coast. Since then the idea has passed its peak but for a period of several years Bob was riding the crest of a big fortune wave that almost forced the business to expand uncontrollably.

The truth is that every basic idea area achieves a peak time when expansion is almost inevitable. At this point the pent-up demand becomes so great that almost anyone entering business during this time period will zoom to great riches. This demand frequently continues for a year or two and then declines slightly. After that time the business will still produce a reasonable return on the investment, but it won't build over-night millionaires. During the peak demand years, however, it's almost impossible to miss creating a giant fortune from almost nothing. When you begin to consider your own fortune building, you must look for ideas with fortune-building potential. This means ideas with so much pent-up demand that you can't help but strike it rich almost immediately. To find these idea areas, simply ask yourself these four simple questions:

1. What areas can I think of that seem to have a large unfulfilled demand right now?

2. Is the current market large enough in this area to offer a chance for profit within one or two months?

3. Will the demand in this area double or triple within a year?

4. Does this area spark people's imagination? Does it create excitement?

Once you decide on an idea area that has a large unfulfilled demand and can answer yes to the last three questions, you probably have something that will make you a million.

Let's look at a few idea areas that have good fortune-building potential right now.

Try One of These Fortune-Building Areas

Some fortune-building areas are better than others in which to begin your hunt for riches. Many areas, as we've seen, have a time period when the pent-up public pressure makes them an automatic gold mine. While not every one of the following will be for you personally, they all offer a good big money opportunity to anyone who will study them carefully and then come up with an "angle" that is hot right now.

Capitalize On The Billion-Dollar Trends

Every era has its bandwagons as public needs and interests change, the economy shifts, or national and international issues fluctuate. The vast majority of people go from one fad or trend to another, spending collectively millions of dollars each time.

Some of today's strong interest trends are alternate energy sources, organic foods, vegetable gardening, storing and preserving food, and silver and gold investments. People's interest currently has reached an almost fever pitch with a pot of gold waiting for anyone who can successfully satisfy a demand related to these areas.

With alternate energy sources, for instance, many people and companies are now working hard to come up with some workable way to use solar power economically. The company that eventually markets a small efficient economical unit will make millions. As the power shortage has grown, many new companies have also sprung up to manufacture windmills. In the furture, of course, there will be room for many more.

Silver also has made many new millionaires within the past two or three years, since writers and economists have started advising the public that money would continue to decline in value and that savings accounts and most other investments would soon become extremely shaky, while silver would continue to increase in value.

A New York school teacher named Ray J. sensed the uneasy economic trends and decided to cash in on the public's silver interest. Coming to California, he tied in with a local company and began to sell silver bars in the parking lots of several large industrial concerns on pay day. Ray simply passed out a silver brochure one week ahead, then on pay day came back to answer questions and sell silver. The result: landslide sales. It turned out that the average worker was scared to death of losing his savings, didn't trust government, business, or banks any longer and wanted a hedge against the future. Within his peak sales period, Ray sold over a million dollars worth of silver within four short months.

To keep up with the big money trends, you must know what's happening. Read newspapers; ask yourself what areas people seem to be most interested in, and clip newspaper and magazine articles that indicate public needs. Newspapers, for instance, have recently run thousands of articles on the energy shortage and the need to develop alternate sources—this should trigger you to the coming big money potential in this area. Besides clipping from newspapers and magazines, observe what's happening around you, then jot down in a notebook any trends you observe along with tips to yourself on how to make money. Just one good tip that hits can easily make you a million almost overnight.

Follow the Wealth Building Fads

Over the past twenty years several billion dollars has been pocketed by smart money people who recognized a coming fad. Good examples of these are the hula hoop, water beds and skate boards. The hula hoop, for instance, caught the public fancy overnight. The original manufacturer suddenly received more orders than he could possibly fill and hundreds of other manufacturers jumped in with imitations to capture many millions more in hula hoop profits.

How do you tell what will become a million-dollar fad and what won't? Try thinking of secondary needs that strike a fancy. What does the public need temporarily that it doesn't have now that will create an exaggerated following? A few areas begin to emerge. For instance, many people believe that they aren't getting exaggerated following? A few areas begin to emerge. For instance, many people believe that they aren't getting enough out of life, nor do many have the deep meaningful relationships and experiences they long for. Look, for example, at the former popularity of encounter groups and the success of such books as *I'm OK, You're OK.* One of the areas that might help fulfill this fad need is the "experience" vacation—that is, a vacation where people obtain some meaningful experience. One might, for instance, go on a university-sponsored archeological expedition, or spend a week on a fishing boat off the Alaskan coast helping to haul in the catch or become a member of a New Zealand crew measuring glacial movement.

One company today actually offers vacations like these; they have a long waiting list. This fad currently has a long way to go to reach its peak. Anyone who figures out a different way to give people a really meaningful experience may well cash in big.

Dancing also has recently gone through a long no-touch cycle. But there are currently many indications that touch-dancing with infinite fad variations is on the way back. Arthur Murray made a fabulous fortune on the dance fad during the last several decades and there will be many more made in this same area during the next ten years by anyone who can learn to make the dance trends work for them.

In the toy line we are also overdue for another fad. In the past, skate boards and hula hoops fulfilled the need to participate. Both, for instance, used the entire body. This need still exists and anyone who can come up with a total body participation toy that sparks the mass imagination will automatically create an overnight demand.

Fads can be created to satisfy what is a hidden secondary

need. Sometimes you can find these fad needs by examining idea areas one by one and by listing anything that might temporarily attract an exaggerated following. Take, for example, cooking, gardening and automobiles. A possible cooking fad might be a gadget that tells you when you have cooked certain kinds of meat to rare, medium rare, medium and well done. For gardening, a fad item might be a new kind of sprinkler that waters and fertilizes at the same time; for automobiles, a new kind of horn with an unusual sound, or a radio speaker system in which the sound completely engulfs the driver and passengers.

Explore These Big Opportunity Services

People always need service. The trick in establishing your fortune-making service is to pick need areas that people will pay for with big cash. The following have good potential: rentals, publicity, franchising, and recreational services.

Rental housing has now come into its own. The cost of owning a home has skyrocketed. Financing cost has risen astronomically and many young couples simply don't want the work involved in owning their own home. In many areas, however, rental housing is difficult to find and the need is for a service that links the potential renter with good housing. Some rental services do exist, but so far no one has merchandised this concept in such a way as to attract a massive number of customers. Some people, of course, have made big money offering this service, but the potential here is still largely untapped.

Tim H., for instance, decided to move his family to a nearby suburban community and rent for at least the first year. Unfortunately, after several weeks Tim, a Denver factory worker making only $8000 a year, failed to find one suitable house or a real estate agency that could really help him. Exasperated, Tim realized there must be many other people in the same boat. After thinking it over for some time he decided that maybe this area could use a really good rental service agency. Tim put notices on bulletin boards, advertised in the local papers, made announcements at parent-teacher meetings and did everything else he could think of to attract rental listings. To make his service really irresistible to home owners he guaranteed that he would start paying rent the minute a home owner signed up. He counted on the overdemand for rentals at premium rates to enable him to offer this kind of guarantee and still make money. As it turned out, he was 100 percent right. Owners happily gave him their rental needs since he took on all the risks and headaches. Within a short time Tim had attracted over 500 listings, more than anyone else in the area. His personal income at this point topped $5000 a month. He then purchased a nearby 100-acre ranch, put in a huge swimming pool and started living in the style that he had long felt he deserved.

Publicity services also offer almost unlimited possibilities. Few small businesses take advantage of publicity, yet frequently it can do more for a business than any amount of advertising.

For instance, Billie C., a housewife, decided to work part-time selling real estate because she needed extra money to help pay the increased rent and skyrocketing food bills. Billie made many sales, but didn't enjoy selling. She did, however, like to write and had always longed to work on a newspaper. One day she decided she could combine the two talents. Real estate people needed publicity to attract potential buyers, yet few of them explored this form of advertising. Billie then approached her own boss and explained how publicity could supplement and increase his advertising effectiveness while reducing his overall cost. After listening to her argument he decided to try her new service for three months. He was in the process of launching a condominium development and needed to attract potential buyers.

Billie hired a photographer and took pictures of the realtor and the builder at the development. She also wrote several stories on the realtor himself, his backing of a Little League team, and his fight to obtain a park for the city. These she managed to place as new items in 15 local newspapers. This treatment made the realtor an instant local celebrity and brought him tremendous attention. Within two months she managed to pick up six more accounts and by the end of the year had contracts totaling almost $50,000 a year.

Few small businessmen can afford to pay advertising agency rates for this service, yet most could benefit tremendously from it. The trick here is to put together all the possible ideas about a client that would be considered news: athletic team sponsorship, community participation, stories about how the business got started, contests and more. Write these up as news stories copying the style of printed news items, then send them along with a picture to all of the local area newspapers.

Franchising: Many agencies today help companies franchise their business throughout the United States. There is still, however, a tremendous need for this service among small businessmen who want to grow. Anyone with a little knowledge of franchising and a certain amount of business savvy can operate as a franchise broker. Many colleges and universities today offer franchising courses which will help get you started. Check with several nearby ones and take the class that best suits your needs.

Recreational services: Tour arranging has become tremendously big business today because people love to travel with other people. Companies arrange foliage tours, European train tours, Mexican camping tours and many others.

Bill W., for instance, thought recreational vehicle tours through Canada, Europe and North Africa might be popular. He arranged to rent RVs in each area, hired local tour guides and ran ads in recreational vehicle and camping and outdoor magazines. The Canadian tour (his first one) attracted 40 couples at $500 a couple and ran up overhead expenses of $8000. Bill pocketed a cool $12,000 on this one and was on his way to success. He currently sponsors many fabulous tours all over the world and takes home a yearly income in excess of $100,000.

There are, of course, many other services that can be tapped for big money. A few include: arranging weekend ski cabins rentals, helping people exchange homes, and helping to create personal careers.

Simply sit down and decide what kind of service you can perform that people really need. Think of today's pressures. Do people need help finding a good job? Do they need planned recreation? Do they need personal investment counseling? What else? After you decide on a service need, sit down and work out all the details of launching that particular business.

Choose Old Areas With Big Fortune Potential

Many old areas which in the past have created hundreds of millionaires still attract tremendous attention and currently offer almost unlimited possibilities. A few of these are: skiing, golf, tennis, motorcycles, and recreational vehicles.

Skiing, for instance, has been around a long time now, yet it continues to attract tremendous attention and offer many additional opportunities every season. The trick is to take a new approach to the old theme. For instance, a young ambitious, highly motivated East Coast executive named Mark F. took over a ski resort in the Catskills that was just about to go broke. The ski lifts were in terrible shape; practically no one patronized the restaurant; the entire place needed a complete overhaul. For the first few months after Mark took over, his brother handled the cooking while Mark himself washed dishes and acted as maitre d'. Instead of selling skiing, the brothers decided to merchandise leisure-time recreation, concentrating on developing the hotels, restaurants, second-home developments, and summer trade. As a result, they literally turned the resort around in a few months and the company itself soon had sales close to $100 million.

Some skiing ideas that could be explored are: a series of ski touring huts four or five miles apart where people could stay for the night, ski cabin weekends for singles, party ski trains or party ski buses.

Golf, also, had attracted tremendous interest for many years, yet it still offers unlimited potential for creating new fortunes: golf classes, competition for juniors, overseas golf tours, celebrity golf clinics and similar enterprises.

Tennis offers similar possibilities: tennis clubs, lessons for housewives, tennis tours, a singles' tennis resort, a tennis condominium, tennis exercise clubs and more.

Motorcycles: The motorcycle business has changed tremendously over the last ten years. Today affluent young businessmen have taken up the sport in droves. This flow of new money has created tremendous opportunities: motorcycle rentals, singles' motorcycle tours, a motorcycle resort, condominium recreational developments for motorcycle enthusiasts and many more.

Recreational vehicles: recreational vehicle sales have continued to rise since the early 1960s, and although today huge firms including General Motors are involved in the field, there are still millions of dollars just waiting for the taking. Recreational vehicle resorts, recreational vehicle tours, do-it-yourself recreational vehicle kits, and all sorts of recreational vehicle accessories are only a few possibilities.

There are many other fields that offer big opportunity. Simply look around for areas with continuing popularity that still attract large sums of money; then try to think up interesting ideas that would interest significant groups of people. After you've come up with a number of side businesses, sort out your ideas and pick the best ones to put into action.

Try These Smart Money Sales Opportunities

Many sales opportunities exist today that can make you rich almost overnight. You must, of course, pick sales fields that take advantage of current trends or represent areas that are just starting to become popular. Possibilities here include do-it-yourself housing, discount food plans, and semi-pyramid sales.

Do-it-yourself housing offers real possibilities for anyone looking for a sure-fire fortune. The price of housing has skyrocketed; labor costs account for one-half to two-thirds of the total price. As a result, you'll find a tremendous market for a low-cost do-it-yourself home package.

With a product like this, it is probably best to find someone who is already in production and offer to set up a sales organization in your area.

Discount food plans also offer great opportunity. After all, nothing concerns the American housewife as much today as the cost of food. As a result there is a wide open market for anyone who can offer a food plan that will allow one to eat better for less. You might offer a buying cooperative, a cooperative farm project, a farm-to-consumer plan store, or any other well thought-out ideas that will do the job.

Set up your own sales force and encourage each salesman to recruit others. You can sell almost anything this way: indoor house plants, Christmas cards, toys, cosmetics and jewelery. You will find many products available for sale from *Salesman's Opportunity* and similar magazines. Pick these up at your local news stand.

From here on you can think up your own. What you want to do is to sell something that takes advantage of current trends and rising growth.

Find Your Gold Mine In Distressed Real Estate

Old distressed housing has already made many millionaires and will create hundreds more within the very near future. Indeed, real estate is still one of the better ways to get rich quick because value continues to rise astronomically.

Tom H., for instance, turned $1000 into over a million dollars within ten years by buying and selling distressed houses. Tom put his $1000 down on an old house no one else wanted, painted the outside, repaired the foundation, added a room and sold it for an $8000 profit. He then took this $8000 and bought a small four-unit apartment house on which he made (after alterations) $22,000. He then continued buying small apartment houses over the next few years realizing $15,000 to $30,000 on each one.

The trick in buying distressed real estate is to drive the buying price down so your improvements will create a big increase which you can pocket. What makes this possible is that a few easily repairable defects often drive the selling price down many thousands of dollars. You must then look for a generally sound house which has excellent selling points, but one in which the owner has neglected to repair the "major selling price increasers." In appraising a house for potential fortune building make sure that you have the following:

Large bedrooms and closets

Good floors

Good laundry facilities

A good roof

A good main foundation

A good basement (if any)

The following items can increase the price astronomically when repaired:

Outdated fixtures: old-looking electrical fixtures and faucets are inexpensive to replace, yet new-looking replacements update a place tremendously.

Peeling and cracking paint: Paint is relatively cheap, but it makes the house much more attractive and valuable to a potential buyer.

A sagging porch. Sagging porches pull the value down tremendously, yet generally have nothing to do with the basic house and can be fixed cheaply.

Age: The older the better as long as the house is in good condition. The inspection slip (posted somewhere in the house) will tell you how old that house really is. You can then use age as a bargaining point to drive the price down.

To determine what you should offer, first take 10 percent off the offering price (since no seller ever expects to get what he asks); then subtract an additional five percent for each of the preceding items. Subtract an additional five percent for each 10 years of age over 20 years.

Buying distressed housing actually is a very specialized field. The book *How I Turned $1000 Into Three Million in Real Estate in My Spare Time*, by William Nickerson (Simon and Schuster), will help increase your expertise.

Set Up a Big Money Action Plan

Once you finally decide what you are going to do, begin immediately. If you have drawn up a written prospectus as we suggested earlier, you now know who your customers are, something about your potential costs and a few of the market possibilities. Now sit down and actually lay out your big money action plan. If you intend to develop real estate, draw up a need list and follow your need steps one by one.

Rick G., for instance, was a retired telephone company employee who had retired on a $6000 a year pension. Since this hardly covered food and rent, Rick decided to open an amusement center for children consisting of a bumper car concession and a pinball machine building. He then spent several years accumulating a $22,000 nest egg through moon-lighting, present income accumulation and borrowing.

Even then, for awhile Rick just couldn't seem to get started. Finally he sat down, took stock of himself and decided that if he didn't come up with a definite plan he'd never start his business. He listed, on a blackboard, every possible step he could think of. This included obtaining the licences, insurance, having the electricity turned on, ordering the units, leasing the lot, installing the lights and supervising construction, among other things. He then arranged them in the order that seemed logical. With each item he tried to complete all details before going on to the next. By the time he reached the bottom his first fortune-making business was ready to launch.

In setting up your own big money action plan you should first list every possible step on a blackboard or a piece of paper. Try to include every detail. Don't exclude anything just because you believe it might be silly.

Next combine those that are similar and eliminate any that are absolutely unnecessary.

Arrange those left in some logical order.

Finally follow them one by one. Make sure you complete all details of one step before going on to the next.

By following this procedure diligently, you will almost automatically launch yourself to a big-money fortune with no pain.

How to Utilize the Magic of Newspaper Publicity

Newspaper publicity can (as we've seen before) multiply the results of your fortune-building activities many times since this publicity can reach thousands at almost no cost. You should, therefore, utilize publicity to launch your business and to help it along every step of the way.

As we've already mentioned, newspapers are always looking for items of interest to their readers and will report on business openings, community involvement, and interesting employees. You should use your imagination and try to get almost everything you do into the newspaper.

Rand H., for instance, decided to open a small Mexican restaurant near a medium-sized city. First Rand had a picture taken and wrote up a news release on the opening. He then sent out a release and a picture on a waitress beauty contest (nine local papers picked this up). He also asked several local artists to display their paintings in his restaurant (eight newspapers reported on this). Rand even offered a round trip to Disneyland as a prize to the 5000th customer to buy a meal at his restaurant. Seventeen newspapers picked this item up along with a picture of the customer's family accepting the airplane tickets. He continued this practice throughout his business career, often placing 100-plus stories and pictures every year.

As a result, the restaurant became far better known than if Rand had used direct advertising alone. For your own business, simply use your imagination to think of news items you feel people in your community would like to read about.

To decide which to write up, watch the news stories and pictures in your local newspapers, clipping those that interest you; then decide how you could develop similar stories about your own business. This one device alone will supply you with almost unlimited ideas.

How To Use Continuing Capital Building As Your Big Money Path To Automatic Wealth

Capital building can easily launch you on your way to an initial big-money fortune, but don't stop at your first venture, because the capital-building methods taken up in this book can build big money capital throughout your entire fortune-building career. This will create expansion many times faster than any other method. In other words, out of every dollar taken in you should, as we did in the beginning, set aside a certain percentage for future expansion.

Ben W. was a New York insurance company employee until he began a catalog mail order business on $4000 capital. He built it into a $4 million a year operation in three years. At that point Ben decided that if he could create capital fairly rapidly from his original small income, he could escalate this capital accumulation enormously from an established business. He then began to take ten percent from his gross profit every month and deposit it in a savings account. At the end of the first year he had put aside $7500; by the second, $35,000. Ben used this money as a down payment on two small apartment houses. As the cash began to come in from these, he took ten percent from this profit and added it to the capital accumulation bank account. He then invested this money in a small business building, continuing from then on to plow back a percentage of the profits which he invested in whatever business looked promising at the time. By the end of the sixth year, Ben owned 15 apartment houses, three business buildings, a car agency and two large supermarkets.

For your own business, consider this capital savings program as a basic expense similar to rent, salaries, heat and other overhead. In the beginning, set an arbitrary amount ($50 to $200); then as you start making a profit, change that to a set percentage (generally from 10 to 20 percent).

As we did originally, take this money out first every month before you pay bills and put it in the bank. Again, do not touch this money for any purpose except further business expansion. This will automatically give you expansion cash when you need it. You will then, in spite of yourself, be forced to move on to big money wealth.

POINTS TO REMEMBER

1. Keep a notebook regularly and write down in general terms how you intend to create a big money fortune.

2. Start as small as possible, hold back some money and expand at least two times during the first year. This creates the idea that you're really going strong.

3. Look for ideas with fortune-building potential in areas with great public need or interest.

4. Once you decide what you're going to do, make up an action plan and start immediately.

5. Create news items for your business and obtain as much newspaper publicity as possible.

6. Continue to build capital by taking a fixed percentage out of your business first every month before paying any other bills. Set this aside for future expansion.

8
How to Make
the Force of Habit
Pay Off Big

As you begin to put your big money fortune-building activities together, you will need to decide just how you intend to work. You can consciously make every decision as it comes up, starting anew each time, or you can put together a work pattern which you follow over and over until it becomes a habit. After a few tries, each step will become almost automatic, requiring a conscious decision only when you do something different. This method saves a great deal of effort since the very act of considering any work-step requires time and energy.

Think back to when you first began to drive. You did everything slowly and deliberately. You had to think to turn on the key; you had to think to take the brakes off; you had to make a conscious decision when you came up behind a car. That's why you were so cautious. Later on you began to shift some of the operations further back in your mind until you performed them almost unconsciously. Look what happens now: you jump in the car, put the key in and press down on the starter—automatically. Sometimes this becomes such a habit that you don't even realize what you've done. You then go on your way—putting on the brakes, making turns, signaling—

almost without realizing what's happening. Sometimes it's possible to drive miles without making any conscious effort. You have in effect shifted this function of your life over to "automatic pilot."

That is exactly what you must do with wealth building. You must, in the beginning, begin to build standard big money methods and habits that will carry you along to a giant fortune almost without effort.

Sam Q., for instance, a former Philadelphia furniture worker, retired on a small $6000 a year pension. He soon found this inadequate, and in desperation set out to launch his own cabinet shop. Being methodical, Sam also decided that it would be much easier if he could make fortune building as much of a habit as possible. He first established a habitual savings program, taking $100 a month from his pension every month. He then set up a one-hour idea and planning session in the morning and a one-hour get-started-in business session in the afternoon. Sam scheduled these sessions for the same hour each day and, to make them as automatic as possible, refused to let any other task take over the alloted time. During the morning hour he simply worked on ideas. In the afternoon he handled the chores necessary to begin business—made necessary phone calls, gathered information, picked up supplies and did anything else required to launch the business. After a few months, both the savings program and work sessions became absolutely automatic and by the end of the year, Sam had raised the necessary money. He had also completed all pre-business details including licenses, sign permits and shop leases. By turning the money saving, planning and work into daily habits, Sam simply let the routine carry him along until the business almost launched itself automatically. The cabinet shop was a success right from the beginning and was soon grossing over $100,000 a year. At this point Sam hired three men to run the shop itself and came in a couple of hours a day to make sure that everything was going smoothly.

How To Make Big Money Habits Work For You

To make your fortune building as painless as possible you simply start with your present already established habits and tag on chores that you find useful in your fortune-building business.

The first step is to list your already established habits. Let's look at a few typical ones:

Get up at 7:00 AM every morning

Spend 30 minutes driving to work

Have coffee at 10:15 AM and 3:15 PM

Drive home 30 minutes every day

Read the paper 25 minutes before dinner

Watch television two hours

Go to bed at 10:00 PM

Next make a list of the things you need to accomplish:

Need to find a name for your business

Need to make needed business decisions

Need to investigate city and county business ordinances

Need to find supplies

Need to work out advertising program

After that try to match your habits to the tasks that need doing. Why, for instance, can't you think about your business while driving to work? You can certainly develop a few business names and work on your advertising program. As soon as you get to work, take out your notebook and jot down your thoughts on paper. Do this regularly every morning and it soon becomes automatic. You can readily do the same thing while reading the evening newspaper or watching television.

If, for instance, you are looking for a business name, let what you hear and see on television trigger your imagination. If you're trying to work out a problem, clip anything from your newspaper that might apply. In this way, by utilizing habits already in force, you can get started almost immediately.

Bill W., a low-paid bus driver, dreamed of owning a cabin cruiser and a large house on a nearby lake. One day Bill determined that he'd try to market a new game he had invented several years earlier, utilizing the "existing habit" method.

First he sat down and decided what habits he had already established. He spent twenty-five minutes both morning and evening driving to and from work. He read the paper twenty-five minutes, looked over magazines for half an hour and then watched TV for a couple of hours each day.

Bill next made a list of projects he needed to accomplish. He needed a name and he needed to work out game details. During his newspaper and magazine reading and TV-watching time Bill jotted down anything that looked good in a special notebook. Within a week he came up with over 300 names, among the Goldfrab, Penny Pincher and Beat the Bank. In the end he decided that Penny Pincher best expressed his basic idea.

During the 25 minutes required to drive to work he began to work out the game details. The minute he pulled in the parking lot he took out his notebook and jotted down his thoughts. As a result he completed all details in a three-week period. To obtain supplies and do the actual work, of course, he needed additional time, but Bill accomplished the thinking part during a habit period that he would ordinarily waste.

How To Zoom To Riches On The Big Money-Saving Habit

One of the most important habits utilized by any big money fortune builder is the money-saving habit. We discussed in Chapter 2 taking money from your income for a capital building fund; this is important. Now, however, **you** must try to make all capital building as automatic as possible. This means either authorizing someone else to take money from your paycheck before you have a chance to touch it or taking out the same amount on the same date month after month until saving becomes second nature. With this same date saving method (once deeply ingrained), you literally won't be able to stop saving and will go on adding to your fortune-building fund almost forever.

Jack T., for instance, is a businessman who built a $1200 nest egg into a $5 million dollar real estate fortune, Jack began by taking $50 a month from his then small government paycheck. He at first set aside a definite amount each month, but failed to establish a definite savings date. The first month Jack deposited on the fourth; the second month about the fifteenth; the third month about the fifth; the fourth month he forgot to make a deposit at all, simply because saving was not yet the ingrained habit. After that he remembered the next month but forgot the month after that. By the end of the year Jack had saved only $300.

At this point he realized that unless he did something immediately he would never accumulate his much-needed fortune-building capital. From then on he decided that not only would he set aside $50 every month, but he'd do it on the third of each month. As the months went by savings became almost a ceremony and Jack didn't feel right that day until he had made his deposit. By the end of the year Jack had accumulated $600, had by then deeply ingrained the saving habit in his method of operation, and used it from then on over the next 15 years to establish a huge big money capital-building fund.

How To Make Good Work Habits Your Path To Great Wealth

Good fortune-building work habits generally mean uniformity and regularity. If you are trying to launch a business, for instance, you must write letters, make phone calls and handle a thousand other tasks. Each of these chores, however, can be turned into habits quickly by establishing a definite work time each day. Even if you're tied up on another job at this point you can set aside an hour or two each night or every Saturday.

Most fortune builders find that the more definite they can make this time period, the more work they accomplish. Several utilize a kitchen timer, setting it when they start and stopping when the bell rings. After a few times, these work periods become habitual and deeply ingrained.

You can, of course, do several things to make the habit itself more effective. First, expect a definite amount of work from yourself during each particular time period. If you are working 30 minutes a day, for instance, and have ten letters to do, set yourself a goal of three letters every time period. If you don't accomplish these goals at first, keep working until you do. The important point is to simply set yourself a work goal and keep at it until you reach that goal. Once you do, immediately set new ones.

In addition, to do more, try to group similar chores. Time managers find that each time you change a task you need a certain warmup or adjustment time.

If, for instance, you write a few letters, make a few phone calls, then stop and look up information you will be less efficient than if you spent an hour writing letters, thirty to forty minutes making phone calls and a similar time period looking up information.

Besides, not all work has the same importance. Suppose you need to write three letters about supplies, call about a new plastic process and make an appointment with a potential backer. You then sit down at your desk and start with the first task on your list. By the end of your work period you have written only one letter and called about the plastic process. The really vital task, making an appointment with a possible backer, remains uncompleted. Next day you start at the top of the list again and work your way down. By the end of the day the backer call still hasn't been made.

To unclog this bottleneck and get the most done in the

available time you must classify tasks as to most important, next in importance and so forth. You then must start with the most important task and work your way down the list.

Bill M., for instance, is a big money fortune builder who ran a $1500 nest egg into a $10 million dollar real estate empire. Bill found in the beginning that he hardly accomplished anything for the time spent. Examining his work day closely, he realized that in many cases he utilized his time for unimportant tasks, leaving the important ones undone. Plugging this loophole, Bill soon began churning out the essential work and in a short time had bought five properties which eventually brought a good $100,000 profit—all made possible because Bill learned to handle the essential tasks easily in the time available.

How Smart Money Daily Habits Can Make You Rich

If you intend to create a giant fortune you must realize now that what you do every day is vitally important. After all you really produce the final big money result by linking together each day's efforts in one long chain. Individually, of course, each habit has little impact, but taken all together and performed regularly they create a big money power that makes your eventual fortune almost inevitable. Let's look now at some of the most important:

Establish a Daily Notebook Time

The daily notebook habit is without a doubt one of the most useful daily habits you will ever utilize. Consider it the key that unlocks your imagination and provides you almost automatically with unlimited amounts of information. Into this notebook should go any ideas you have, useful pieces of conversation, information gained from radio, television and magazine articles, and anything else. You might want to jot down, for instance, a possible marketing program, an interesting way to advertise, possible new products, or perhaps simply a way to make your stationery more attractive. Put in it anything that might be useful to your fortune-making business. It is details like these that will eventually propel you to success.

Jack C., for instance, a low-paid Washington D.C. government clerk, started the notebook habit early in his fortune-building career. In the beginning, Jack decided that he would spend ten minutes every morning jotting down ideas. He would then carry the notebook throughout the day, noting anything of interest that came up or popped into his head.

First, Jack heard two secretaries mention the problem of producing a good clear unmarred copy for extremely particular bosses. This intrigued him, so he jotted the idea down. He did not know what to do with this snatch of conversation at that point. Several days later Jack read about an invention which automatically corrected copy by typing over any mistake. He jotted down the inventor's name. He later looked up the telephone number and noted that also. After that, any time he visited a government office he made a note of anyone who controlled the purchase of supplies. Whenever possible, he made notes about that person's likes and dislikes. Next to one secretary's name, for instance, he noted "doesn't like to talk before 10 AM;" for another, "likes to be told how nice she looks." This material might be useful, he reasoned, if he decided to go into this business. Over the next month he also jotted down ideas on how to advertise, ideas for improving the original product, ideas for reaching more secretaries and so on.

Three months later Jack called the inventor, made an appointment and offered to distribute the product in the Washington D.C. area. This offer was immediately snapped up. Jack then passed out samples to every secretary listed in his notebook. He asked that they simply try it and report to him how they liked it. He also asked for additional names of anyone they thought might be interested in trying out the product.

For a couple of weeks nothing happened, then suddenly the orders started to pour in. By the end of the third month Jack had sold over $15,000 worth of the product just on the basis of the few ideas he had jotted down in his notebook.

From here he went on to set up a number of different office product lines and establish a distributorship that eventually grossed well over $3 million dollars a year—all because Jack developed the notebook habit and used it to full advantage.

Establish a Daily Problem Work Time

In addition to a daily workbook habit, every big money fortune builder needs daily problem-solving time. Jack C., for instance (our former government clerk) decided soon after he had began his notebook habit that he also needed some time every day to wrestle with the many problems that continued to pop up. He discovered, for instance, that many secretaries had an extreme aversion to new salesman and some even refused to talk to him the first time he sat foot in their office. Jack put this problem to himself in several daily sessions and decided that if they didn't like salesmen, then he simply wouldn't come in as a salesman. Instead he would just walk in, hand out samples and request that they try it. He reasoned that the product was so good that they would be forced to come back to him later to reorder. His assumption proved correct. Orders for almost $8000 a week poured in for the first six months, later settling down to provide Jack a $75,000-a-year personal income.

Establish a Regular Daily Reading Program

Besides the notebook and problem-solving habits, it is also extremely important for every fortune builder to establish some way to acquire good problem-solving information. As a result, many fortune builders throughout their careers utilize daily reading and information-gathering sessions. During this period they gather material from magazines, pamphlets, books and anything else that helps them build toward a golden future.

Jack C., for instance, felt that reading was one of the big money keys that would help him grow and develop. Early he established a 5:00 PM to 5:30 PM reading time each day.

Generally, he pinpointed a problem, then acquired books or magazines that might help solve this problem. One of his troubles, he discovered, was in managing his time. He then checked three time management books out of a nearby library and carefully poured through them for 20 minutes a day, taking notes and jotting down anything he felt might be useful. As a result he soon began utilizing many time-saving devices and constantly improved his own work efficiency.

During the course of the year, Jack learned a great deal about management, advertising, accounting and much more—all of which later found their way into his fortune-making ventures.

In setting up your own program, simply look for books which you feel will be useful to your own immediate future. A few you might want to start with are:

The Management of Time, McKay, Prentice-Hall.

How I Made $1,000,000 in Mail Order, Cossman, Prentice-Hall.

The Complete Layman's Guide to the Law, Hanna, Prentice-Hall.

You Can Become a Super Salesman, Kenian, Drake.

How to Start and Manage Your Own Small Business, Gardiner, McGraw-Hill.

Beyond Survival, a Business Owner's Guide to Success, Danco, Prentice-Hall.

Franchise Opportunities, A Business of Your Own, Drake.

Set Up A Daily Paperwork Control Habit

Paperwork bogs down more big money fortune builders than almost anything else since it's involved in almost every kind of activity. Again, good daily habits can bail you of this money and time waster. In analyzing lost time, management consultants discovered that most people handle a single piece of paper many times before finally getting rid of it. In a recent case study, for instance, a fortune-building executive who received a memo from a supplier first looked over the memo then put it in the basket for action. Next day he read the memo again and made a note to himself, then moved it on to the supplier's basket. Next he reread it and moved it to the answer box. Finally he decided the memo didn't need answering so he threw it away—a total time waste of 33 minutes.

The secret is to carefully examine each piece of paper initially. Throw those away that have no usefulness, then decide immediately what to do with the others. If something needs a short note, jot down the answer right there. If you intend to file it, do that; if it needs more work or a long answer, then put it in a special basket reserved for that purpose; but don't put that piece of paper down until you've taken it as far as possible in a short time. Actually it's also good policy to answer all longer letters the same day they arrive. This keeps you up to date, makes all work flow smoothly and creates a tremendous impression on other people.

How To Turn Letter Writing Habits Into Your Personal Gold Mine

Probably nothing pays off more than good daily letter writing habits. Every day of your life you continually come across (in your reading) potential new products, new ideas, new processes, and people who can really help. The trick to turning these reading encounters into eventual cash is to jot down a note the minute you see something that strikes you, then later write for more information. This information, you will find, can sometimes be worth millions.

Gage B., for instance, always utilized this method quite effectively. Gage, a former $8000 a year Indianapolis bottling plant worker, used capital-building methods to propel himself into the ownership of a $3 million-dollar-a-year grounds mainte-nance firm.

First Gage went to the library and asked the reference desk for the business edition of the Standard Rate and Data Guide. This listed all the business magazines in his field including *Grounds Maintenance, Lawn Garden Marketing, Outdoor Power Equipment, Turf Grass Times, Weeds, Trees, and Turf, Western Landscaping, Landscape Industry, Home and Garden Supply Merchandiser* and others.

One of the big problems in his area, Gage knew, was leaf removal during the fall. In one issue of *Grounds Maintenance* magazine he found a number of different methods along with the names and addresses of suppliers. Since he had established the letter-writing habit long ago, he simply sat down and wrote for all available information from both the manufacturers and the authorities listed in the articles. From the material received Gage eventually established a leaf removal sideline that grossed an extra $125,000 the first year. Through this same letter-writing habit he learned about weed control, how to develop an inspection and improvement system, how to service his equipment more efficiently, how to cut watering costs, how to spot diseased plants and a lot more. In addition, the authorities he corresponded with often dropped by to see Gage when passing through his area, frequently passing on valuable tips that helped improve his business. All in all, Gage estimated, his letter-writing habit brought in an additional $250,000 every year.

The trick here is to decide what magazines or newspapers affect your field. Like Gage, you can look up business trade journals in the Standard Rate and Data Guide; also, add a good financial paper like *The Wall Street Journal,* your local paper, perhaps *Business Week* magazine, and anything else you feel might be useful. Scan these in your letter-writing period and write letters to persons or companies who might provide useful information. Over the years this habit will pay off big in hundreds of ideas you can convert into cash.

How To Millionize the Newspaper and Magazine Clipping Habit

This is very similar to the letter writing habit but with a

vital difference. Every fortune builder (as we've already seen) must have a steady stream of ideas and information coming in at all times if he intends to really maximize his income.

For instance, a former high school bus driver named Bill S. turned a run-down restaurant into a million dollar gold mine. Bill did it primarily by utilizing the clipping habit. First he decided he needed to bring in all the information he could find. As in the case of Gage B., Bill S. looked up all the magazines pertaining to his business in the Standard Rate and Data Guide at the library and then subscribed to *Dining, Drive In, Fast Service, Fast Food, Food and Equipment Product News, Hospitality,* and several local newspapers. Then, as with the letter-answering habit, Bill regularly read all incoming material every day. Instead of writing letters, however, he clipped anything that looked promising. Over a two month period he had found an item on a circus wagon children's menu which eventually resulted in a $1000-a-month increase in his family business. An unusual mobile salad wagon which was wheeled directly to each table resulted in an additional $1500 a month. A specialized restaurant entrance wine storage area allowing customers to select a wine of their choice brought about a $4000-a-month wine sale increase over a six-month period. This newspaper and magazine clipping habit, Bill estimated, resulted in at least a $50,000 increase the first year.

To utilize this habit properly, Bill found he had to clip every day, placing the useful idea in a special box. At least once a week he held an idea session, going over every item in the box to see if it could fit into and improve his existing business. At the end of each session he selected the two best ideas to try for a two-month period. At the end of two months he kept those that really made money and dropped those that didn't.

How To Multiply Your Fortune Building Habits

Habits, as we've seen, can make vast differences along your path to great riches. Some habits will zoom you along almost without effort. Others won't seem to make any difference, and others will actually block your way to big money.

To multiply your good fortune-building habits, however, you must take the habits just mentioned in this chapter and begin working them into your daily schedule. First try each a week or two, retaining those that really seem to work for you, dropping those that don't. In addition, you should take stock of those habits you have now that act as a hindrance and drop them entirely.

You might, for instance, have gotten into the habit of stopping too long for coffee breaks, working on projects that don't make any difference to your progress, talking too long on the phone and others. These will become apparent as you go along. Simply make a list of the ones you wish to get rid of and give yourself a progress rating every day. This added attention will help eliminate these habits as you go along.

Next you must continue to look for and add good habits as you find them. When you discover a good one, simply jot it down in your notebook and try to integrate it into your daily life. A good place to find these habits are in general magazines and in specialized books dealing with how to make money.

A few sources that you will find useful for this purpose are:

How To Be Rich, J. Paul Getty, Playboy Press.

Grow Rich With Peace of Mind, Napoleon Hill, Fawcett.

Your Infinite Power To Be Rich, Murphy, Parker Publishing Co.

The Young Millionaires, Armour, Playboy Press.

How To Think Like a Millionaire and Get Rich, Hill, Parker Publishing Co.

Magic Mind Secrets For Building Great Riches Fast, Hicks, Parker Publishing Co.

(This habit should be combined with the daily reading program habit mentioned earlier in this chapter.)

In general, potential wealth builders have found the following habits extremely useful in helping to acquire a big money fortune: habitual risk taking, continuing education, time saving, decision reviewing, and standing behind what you do and more.

Stanley R., for instance, was an $11,000-a-year railroad employee. Stanley found himself constantly in debt and couldn't seem to make enough money to pay bills. One day he took himself in hand, put together an $11,000 capital nest egg, and began a citywide parcel delivery service. After the first couple of years in which the business increased steadily to $85,000 a year, Stanley decided that his own personal habits as a businessman could be utilized to make even more money.

First, Stanley began utilizing the notebook habit, jotting down potential money-making habits from conversations, reading, the radio, TV and other sources. Next he picked out three which he wanted to integrate into his personal life: promptness, standing behind what he did, and acquiring more knowledge.

After that he resolved to make being on time a habit. This included appointments, customer pickups, business meetings and everything else. Stanley found implementing this resolution to be extremely difficult at first, but after three weeks he began to really enjoy operating his business on a precise schedule. At first nothing happened; then suddenly orders begin to pick up almost without explanation. Curious, he asked a customer why he had suddenly started throwing more business his way.

"I can depend on you," was the reply. "I know that if you say you'll pick up at 4:00 pm, that's exactly what you'll do. And believe me, this promptness means money in the bank to me."

Next, he decided to stand firmly behind everything he did as a habitual way of doing business. The second week after putting this new policy into effect he received a complaint that he had cost a client $1000 because he had failed to deliver the same day as promised. Stanley promptly made out a check for $1000 and sent it along with an apology. He also promised to make good any mistake from then on. Not only did he keep this client's business, but it actually increased by almost $2000 over the next five months. In addition, once Stan made this policy a habitual part of his business he found this one habit alone brought in a yearly bonus of over $50,000.

In line with his habit of acquiring knowledge, Stanley took out subscriptions to several business magazines and began a regular business-related reading program.

First he read an article on a firm similar to his that had painted their vehicles outlandish colors to attract attention. He decided this was a great idea and over the next three weeks painted all his trucks with bright pink polka dots. The result was almost instant recognition. In his reading about tax law, Stanley found several ways to save on taxes, and in a time management article, several ways to cut route and personal desk time. Overall, he estimated this information-acquiring habit brought in at least an additional $70,000 each year.

How To Discover Which Wealth-Building Habits Work For You

All habits, of course, won't work equally well, yet a few will seem like they were tailor made for you. Simply take any potentially useful habit and try it for a full month. At the end of that time rate its effectiveness as a potential money maker on a scale from 0 to 10.

Next rate your overall feeling for that particular habit on a scale from 0 to 10. Do you like it, dislike it, feel that it's working well for you, or what? While you may make money with some habits you don't like, generally those you have a good feeling for are the ones that will produce efficiently for you. Finally, take a look at both ratings. Retain any habit with a rating on both scales above six. Drop any that rate below this point. Those retained are the habits that will help zoom you to a big money fortune in the future.

POINTS TO REMEMBER

1. Habits can make you rich when utilized properly.

2. Make habits work for you by attaching needed chores to already established daily habits.

3. Make savings a deeply ingrained habit by setting aside a definite amount on the same date every month.

4. Increase your work habit efficiency by setting aside definite times every day as work periods, by expecting a certain quantity of work in each time period, by performing the same kinds of chores together and by doing high-priority tasks first.

5. Utilize these habits to increase overall earnings:

   Daily notebook time

   Daily problem solving time

   A daily reading program

   Paperwork control

6. Increase earnings by habitually writing for information.

7. Regularly look for information in newspapers and magazines that will directly increase business income.

8. Look for additional money-making habits everywhere.

9. Determine which habits work well for you by rating them from 0 to 10 as a potential money-maker and 0 to 10 as to how you feel about that particular habit. After a month's trial, retain any habit rated 6 or above.

9

Mine the Full Potential
of Your
Wealth-Building Ideas

From one end of your money-making career to the other, good big money ideas will make the difference between creating a spectacular success or a mediocre one. Think of ideas as a conveyor belt going from where you are to real success. Every time you find a really good idea and put it into use, your big money career will take a sudden spurt.

Ideas, then, are the basic raw material from which you create a giant fortune. In addition, of course, throughout your entire career you will need additional ideas to keep you rolling along.

Most American millionaires actually started with a good basic idea, then utilized the continuing idea route to increase their big money success as they went along.

For instance, the founder of Holiday Inns, Kemmons Wilson, came upon the Holiday Inn idea when he discovered on a trip to Washington D.C. that most motels charged extra for children. This so irritated him that he resolved to go home and build a motel that accepted children free. This was the basic Holiday Inn idea that made him a million. Wilson, however, continued to add to this big money idea base as he went along with such ideas as eliminating the no-vacancy sign, providing a place for the family pet, adding to customer convenience and more. All of these continued to bring additional guests and added considerably to Wilson's overall income.

In another case, Mark Price, who became a millionaire merchandising products and people, found his basic money-making idea one afternoon while talking to a Formica executive. The executive mentioned that while Formica products were selling well, the company had barely cracked the school market. Price then sat down and tried to figure out where Formica might fit into the school program. He reasoned that Formica used on a desk top would make it almost indestructible and practically eliminate replacement costs. With this idea, Price began Desk Tops Incorporated, and traveled across the country talking to school boards about installing plastic-topped desks.

After the basic building years, business boomed, and within a few years Price was able to sell the business for a several million dollars profit.

In still another example, Don Tidwell, who founded Winston Industries and made millions in the mobile home business, constantly searched throughout his career for ideas which would improve his products and increase volume. Every month, for instance, he would buy a stack of home decorating magazines and search through them looking for useful ideas. In one particular magazine he ran across a layout for a cottage with two full baths and wondered if this wouldn't work in a mobile home. The result: the country's first two-bedroom, two-bath mobile home—an idea which made several million dollars in additional profit for Winston Industries.

Go All The Way To Millionize Ideas

Ideas, as we have seen, are the golden keys to big money wealth and are absolutely essential to starting and keeping a big money fortune rolling along. What you must now realize, however, is that the greatest idea in the world is worth absolutely nothing as an idea alone, for to unlock an idea's potential worth, it must be actionized. Once it is actionized, you must then back it with work and follow through, going all out to millionize its potential worth.

Mark Price, for instance, when he came up with the Formica idea, was well established in a secure job at Otis and Company. Once committed, however, he went all the way, quit his job and hit the road to establish his product. "After all," Price says, "You must believe in your own idea and back it all the way."

Once you decide on an idea then, be prepared to throw yourself into it and really back that idea with everything you have.

Be Alert To All Big Money Possibilities

Ideas are everywhere. Unfortunately, however, we aren't ordinarily tuned in to the constant bombardment that's showering us from everywhere. To find them, you generally decide on an area of interest like the restaurant business, mail order, an inventor's service or food storage. Then as you go about your daily business you simply let anything that comes close to your interest area trigger your imagination.

William W. is a former $7000-a-year rental equipment employee who developed a $4000 health food investment into a $500,000 a year business success. William found many of his best ideas in simple everyday living. William had been interested in health and nutrition for several years when he overheard a bookstore owner saying that he had space for rent at the rear of his store but wasn't sure what business would fit well with his own. William pulled out his notebook and jotted down the idea, then began to research it. On investigation it turned out the bookstore had a huge health and nutrition book department and a large "counter-culture" clientel that was interested in this area. This, William felt, was a "plus."

Later, looking through a magazine at his doctor's office William spotted a photo of a sidewalk cafe that utilized wooden telephone company wire spools for tables. He jotted that idea down. Leafing through still another magazine, he discovered a "Toy of the Month Club." This triggered a "Health Food of the Month" idea. A few days after that, with a friend, he entered a basement den that looked like the interior of a mountain cabin. This he noted also.

Starting with the first idea, William negotiated with the bookstore owner for the space and then began to set up his health food business. He brought in logs from a collapsed mountain cabin and set up an attractive rustic mountain sales area at the back of the store. With the telephone spool idea William set up four telephone spool tables directly in front of the cabin front and started serving health food lunches. The toy-of-the-month idea he turned into a health-food-of-the-month, for which he took signups at his store and sent to the customers by mail. As the business progressed, William kept running into ideas which he simply modified to fit his own needs. As a result, his store became an immediate success and eventually grew to a half-million-dollar-a-year business.

Let's look now at a few of the better places to find ideas:

Conventions

Every year hundreds of conventions take place all across the United States, packaging conventions, toy conventions, writer's conventions, secretarial conventions and many more. Each of these offers a gold mine of ideas that can be turned into cash.

At a recent automotive retailers' convention, for instance, speakers told how to set up a mail order department, how to cut warehouse costs, how to increase turnover, how to do a better display job—all ideas which could make you money if you had started an automotive-related business.

To find possible conventions that might interest you, write the Chamber of Commerce of any nearby city and ask for their calendar of coming conventions. You can also find convention calendars in trade journals for particular business fields (look these up at the library in the business edition of the Standard Rate and Data Service). You can also find association addresses for particular fields in the Encyclopedia of Associations at the library reference desk. Simply write to them for their convention date and program for their particular association.

Conversations

General conversation is often one of the better places to turn up ideas. Just listen to the people around you.

Roswell C., for instance, is a big-money fortune builder who turned a $600 nest egg into a six-million-dollar-a-year real estate fortune. He was sitting in a restaurant one afternoon and heard: ... that a new factory was about to move to town and would need the services of several real estate agents to help relocate employees, ... that several homes were about to be sold if the new buyer would move them off their present lots, ... that the city had decided not to build any more parking lots, leaving the field open to someone else. All of this was information and ideas that Roswell felt he could modify to fit his own business.

Roswell C. immediately contacted the president of the company moving to town, explained his service and asked if he could help with their problems of finding new homes for company personnel. The result: the company real estate manager called and asked him to help find homes for 15 middle-level managers. This brought in a $45,000 gross profit. Roswell then called the owner of the homes to be relocated and offered $6000 for both. Reluctantly the owner agreed. Roswell then moved the homes for an additional $2,200, had them painted for $600 and sold them for $22,000 each—a $29,200 profit. Finally he got in touch with the owners of four vacant lots downtown and leased them for $200 a month each. Two months later he sublet the vacant lots to a national parking firm for a yearly profit of $35,000—a total of $109,200 profit in one year's time from just one overheard conversation.

Hobbies

Hobbies not only can launch whole new businesses but sometimes contain ideas that can often be millionized in dozens of ways. One young fortune builder, Mark H., for instance, who frequented craft and hobby shows, often turned up many ideas he could convert into big money. In one instance, he found people using a crayon print process that he modified and turned into a do-it-yourself Christmas card kit marketed by mail. This netted well over $50,000. At another show Mark discovered one hobbyist showing human figures made of cemented rocks. Mark immediately began constructing rock dogs, rock chickens and other animal figures which he marketed to gift stores all over the country for a first year's net profit of $25,000. Mark also had his imagination triggered by an exhibit of tin can art which he promptly turned into fancy Christmas ornaments sold through hundreds of outlets in every state for a first year profit of $35,000. All in all Mark feels he pockets a good $100,000 profit from hobby and craft ideas each year by simply visiting hobby and craft shows and by modifying ideas found there to fit his own commercial needs.

Home and Garden

Home craftsman and home gardeners frequently churn out home-oriented ideas by the dozens. Sam R., for instance, a Los Angeles home craftsman-fortune builder working at home on a $1,000 nest egg, came up with a device which automatically figured compound angles for picture frames, an automatic gate that kept children and dogs in the yard, an easy-to-put-together couch, a backyard adobe oven and many others. All these ideas Sam found he could turn into cash. The picture frame angle computer he marketed through a news release to trade journals around the country. This resulted in $35,000 worth of orders. He also called major department stores in nearby cities offering to demonstrate the frame guide in their hardware departments on weekends. The result: an additional $15,000 in sales during the next four months.

The automatic gate he merchanidised through trade journals, women's magazines and home and garden magazines for $25,000 in sales. The easy-to-make-couch he sold through ads in such home and garden magazines as *Sunset, Better Homes and Gardens* and others. This resulted in $18,500 worth of sales. The adobe oven Sam sold through department stores by contacting the merchandising manager, making an appointment, and then offering to put the ovens in on consignment. The result: $9000 worth of sales.

For the garden, Sam found it possible to merchandise a deep pipe vegetable waterer, an automatic watering system for container plants, a vegetable planting guide and an easy-to-use composting system.

The trick is to simply look for ideas neighborhood home crafters and gardeners have developed and found useful. At first simply collect all ideas; later, go over each and decide what kind of commercial use it might have and how successful it might be when properly merchandised.

Magazines and Newspapers

Magazines and newspapers as we've seen before are virtual idea gold mines. Issues of such magazines as *Popular Science, Popular Mechanics* and others, always contain new product departments, developments and ideas that often can be modified to return big money. For Dave S., a Denver big money fortune builder who turned a $750 nest egg into a $300,000-a-year mail order business, an article on storage in a trailer magazine resulted in the marketing of a portable fold-up storage unit that returned $75,000. A picture of an unusual mirror triggered an idea for a three-way blind spot elimination mirror that returned $85,000.

To find these ideas, Dave goes through these magazines until he finds something he feels has commercial possibilities. He then farms out the manufacturing to three local firms, merchandizes the item through magazine and newspaper ads and his regular mail order catalog.

Business and Professional

Business and professional people frequently originate excellent ideas that can be converted into really big money.

Jerome W., for instance, is a big money fortune builder who has parlayed $600 into a four-million-dollar communications and educational fortune. Jerome says he frequently turned to business and professional sources for his best money-making ideas.

Visiting a doctor's office, for instance, Jerome suddenly realized that this particular doctor handled a tremendous number of patients in an extremely short time. Jerome then discussed the matter with the doctor and discovered that he had worked several years to develop a time management system that really worked. Jerome worked out a royalty arrangement with the doctor, put this method together with material gathered from other sources and sold it to physicians across the country as a short course in time management guaranteed to double their incomes. The need for such a course turned out to be so great that within two years the course produced over $100,000 in income and looked like it would produce big money for a number of years in the future.

Seize Every Wealth-Building Opportunity

A constant supply of good ideas is, of course, absolutely vital to your wealth-building plans. You must, however, not stop with the idea itself, but learn to seize every possible money-making idea wherever you find it and immediately proceed to turn it into a form that will make money. Remember, an idea by itself is static; to turn that idea into big cash you must apply some sort of energy or effort.

Here are the steps you must go through:

First, as we've mentioned, jot down every possible idea.

Don't try to evaluate the idea in the beginning; just make a note of it. You may well find that some idea you initially considered silly will later become your biggest money winner.

Next, schedule an idea application session at least once a week to determine just how you can turn particular ideas into big money. After that, list the steps you must take to put that idea into action. During the next week, then, start with the first step on your action sheet and proceed down the list until you have actually made that idea work.

Sexton H., for instance, was a low-paid New York book-keeper until he managed to turn $5000 into a million-dollar-a-year advertising business. Sexton constantly utilized the idea-action method to make even more money.

During one particular week, Sexton ran into the following ideas: an unusal pair of optical glasses that made the world look rosy; a bumper sticker that said, "This Car Stops At Every Garage Sale," and a lifelike shrunken head.

He then sat down with his notebook during an idea-application session and tried to decide how to turn each into big money.

Sexton started first with the optical glasses and began to toss out possibilities. Some of them were: To use the glasses as a giveaway on the purchase of an unusual foreign car made by one of his clients (the idea was that "you'll get a different view of the world with just one test drive"); using the glasses as an advertising gimmick in connection with a hospital fund-raising drive, and tying the glasses to a savings and loan promotion.

Sexton finally decided to utilize the glasses for the savings and loan company promotion. What the company wanted was a different way of calling attention to themselves. Sexton then invented the slogan: "A Savings Account at First Savings Means a Rosier Future For You." Sexton ran a series of eight ads featuring a five-foot-high picture of the optical glasses and offering a pair to anyone who would open a $10 savings account at First Savings and Loan. He also sent eight people out on the downtown streets, wearing glasses, and exhibiting signs which said "I Found A Rosier Future At First Savings."

Sexton had made a note to make up a huge ten-foot pair of glasses to top off a special counter booth where customers could open new accounts and receive their glasses. Finally he decided to run pictures in the local newspapers of the mayor and other city officials receiving a pair of "rosy" glasses.

Once in motion, the campaign attracted tremendous immediate attention and brought nine inquiries from other savings and loan associations who decided that Sexton was a genius and wanted him to handle their ad campaigns also.

Sexton thought about the "This Car Stops at Every Garage Sale" bumper sticker for awhile, then decided to modify it for a current ad promotion. Sexton was then getting ready for a department store sale campaign, so he simply made up some huge bus bumper stickers which said "This Bus Stops at Handle's Big Clearance Sale." Tied in with other advertising, the campaign created a tremendous sensation, brought Sexton a $12,000 fee, and attracted several new accounts.

With the shrunken heads, Sexton wrote down the ideas of using them for giveaways, of selling shrunken head posters, and of utilizing a shrunken head motif for the interior of an entire store.

Since Sexton had a clothing store pants sale coming up immediately, he decided to turn the whole store into an African jungle with drums, African figures on the walls, spears and similar items. To tie in the heads, he gave a shrunken head to anyone buying a pair of pants. He then made up a TV ad showing an interior shot of the store with both heads and pants floating back and forth. The newspaper ads also tied in to this and, in addition, offered free shrunken heads to the first 50 customers on the sale day. The results: a line to get free heads that stretched all the way around the block—plus over 500 pair of pants sold during the first three days.

The basic principle of turning ideas into big money, Sexton decided, was to seize every possible wealth-building idea, work with it until the idea fits your purpose, decide on the steps needed to make it work, and then proceed to do it as soon as possible.

How to Take Advantage of Your Strong Points

As you become more familiar with the "idea" concept, you'll suddenly start coming up with more good ideas than you can ever possibly use. It is at this point that you must start becoming quite selective. You realize, of course, that all of us do some things much better than others. One man, for instance, works well in wood with his hands, but isn't good at book-keeping. Another likes bookkeeping but hates working with tools. Still another creates ideas well but can't do anything around the house. In other words, not everyone has the same kinds of abilities; yet if we expect our ideas to produce the best possible results, we must match the idea with our individual traits to take advantage of our natural abilities.

Bob P., for instance, an $8000-a-year Kansas City office worker who turned a $5000 nest egg into a three-million-dollar retail empire, begun by utilizing money-building ideas directed along the lines of his greatest talents.

First, Bob sat down and made up a list of over 100 ideas. He could sell jewelry door to door, franchise garage sale methods, go into the restaurant business, help inventors merchandise their ideas, or open a new and different type of toy store on a piece of land he owned next to the freeway.

He then made a list of those things he did well and those he didn't do well. He sold almost everything well; he enjoyed being creative; he liked to decorate; he was a good artist—but he didn't handle people well; he couldn't write well; he couldn't cook, and he didn't organize well.

Bob P. compared each idea with items on his ability list. Jewelry sales would take advantage of his selling ability, but would ignore his creative-artistic-decorative ability. The franchise garage sales would require handling people—one of his negative qualities. The restaurant business would require some cooking, at least in the beginning—another negative quality. The inventor's merchandising idea would primarily require him to work with people—again negative. The toy idea would allow him to sell as well as use his artistic, decorative, and creative abilities.

Despite the fact that he would still have to work with people in the toy business, Bob decided to go ahead. First he designed a crazy-looking building in the form of twelve large multicolored blocks piled one on top of the other. Once completed, this building literally backed up traffic for ten miles because motorists, startled by its appearance, slowed down to get a closer look. Inside, Bob divided the store into several distinct areas. The doll section featured an enchanted tree community with a large squirrel treehouse featuring tiny mail boxes in front of the larger trees. The train section boasted a wild set of train tracks climbing to the top of the building past gigantic snow-topped mountains. Outside large toy figures strolled the walks handing out lollipops to the kids. All in all the store turned out to be a fanciful operation which fully utilized Bob's talents. On opening day over 10,000 people jammed the store and grounds. By the end of the first year Bob had sold well over half a million dollars' worth of toys.

To fully utilize your own abilities as Bob did, list all ideas along with your talents on a sheet of paper. Put down those things you do well as well as things you don't do well. With each idea, then, try to note everything that the idea might entail. Cross off all ideas requiring two or more negative talents or those ideas which do not utilize at least two positive talents. Finally, decided which of the remainder you intend to put into action.

How to See the Entire Big Money Picture

How well a big money idea pays off often depends on how well it fits into your overall big money scheme. To maximize any idea's potential it is necessary to sit down and visualize how that idea fits what you're doing now, or how it will fit into future plans.

For instance, suppose you started a small printing service, added a brochure and design service, started printing signs, and then added a typography service. You then come up with an idea to turn the front portion of your building into a bridal-floral shop. Projecting back, brochures are a natural outgrowth of printing which helps increase total business; so is design, signs and typography. All go together and add to the printing business. A flower shop doesn't. In fact that business will require space you could utilize for the expansion of your principle interests. Projecting out, it seems logical that you should continue adding sidelines that fit into a printing concept. Perhaps an ad agency, a publicity service or a similar operation would feed additional volume to the printing business. You would therefore reject the bridal-floral shop idea.

Next you decide you might like to start a small community newspaper. Projecting back, you could advertise the printing business through the newspaper and could utilize the already existing press to print the newspaper. Projecting forward, you could use an ad agency to create business for the newspaper, and as an arm of the publicity service. The newspaper idea, therefore, fits like a glove.

The trick, then, is to see how any given idea fits into both the past and the projected future of your present business. Somehow any good idea should generate additional business for what you're already doing and blend with any similar business you might want to add later. If it does both of these, you can then proceed with confidence.

How to Set Up a Big Money Think Period

Everybody really needs a big money think period to maximize the effects of their wealth-building activities. In handling any wealth-building business there are so many facets that it's extremely easy to become bogged down in the details and forget to work out far-reaching plans and ideas that automatically push you to success.

Leo R. was a low-paid Atlanta food clerk for many years until he began an extremely successful photographic chain operation on a $4500 capital investment. Midway through the second year Leo found himself spending 14 hours a day handling operational details such as ordering, waiting on customers, displaying, advertising and more. At first his business increased from $1000 a month to almost $6000, then it leveled off and stayed there. Thinking about it, Leo decided that while he was handling day-to-day details well, he had quit planning ahead and looking for additional ideas and promotions that make a business really go. Despite the "time squeeze," Leo determined that he must spend an hour twice a week thinking up ideas, working over old ideas and planning for the future.

During the first month Leo didn't notice any difference. In the second month he sponsored a film and projector contest, dreamed up in his big money think period, that produces a $2000 overall increase in business. As additional ideas went into operation volume began to increase tremendously until by the end of the year the store regularly hit $15,000 a month. Eventually Leo established a ten-store chain which at that point brought him well over $50,000 a year in personal income, sent his children to an expensive private school and began to invest in art and other luxuries.

In setting up your own big money think period you must consider several factors. First you must spend the time necessary to develop your ideas. This means (as we covered in the chapter on habits) setting aside at least one hour a week and making a real ritual of the planning period. Once started you will begin to mentally prepare in advance for the thinking period. This almost unconscious preplanning makes the thinking period itself extremely productive. It's necessary first to think in terms of both large ideas and small ideas. One big money capital builder, for instance, reserves the first 30 minutes for reviewing big ideas like beginning a new advertising program or adding a new addition. The second half he devotes to little ideas—like sign color—or the size of his ads, or moving a counter to the front of the store or something similar. If he doesn't reserve thinking time for the little things, he finds, they simply never get done. In addition in handling all ideas it's extremely important to utilize good brainstorming methods. This means simply sitting down and throwing out everything about the idea that you can dream up, then jotting it down on either a clip board or a blackboard so you can work with it more easily.

If, for instance, you own a bookstore, want to add a children's section, and need to brainstorm the type of carpet you intend to install you might write down:

The carpet or floor covering must:

be kiddy-proof

have bright colors

contain animal patterns

contain fantasy figures

be linoleum tile

use a large central figure

be a color that doesn't show dirt

tie in with some overall children's section pattern

have a star pattern

be made of some new material

be a solid color

be made out of soft foam

be cut out so lights can be inserted directly in the floor

have a railing around it

have a sandbox placed on it

Some of these won't work, but focus on those you like and combine similar ones to make a new list.

The carpet or floor covering must:

tie in with some overall children's section pattern

be kiddy-proof

contain fantasy figures

be linoleum tile

use a large central figure

have bright colors

Using the criteria you have established, you next develop at least three possibilities like these:

1. Put a big green Dr. Seuss's "grinch" on a brown linoleum tile background, tied in with other Dr. Seuss's fantasy figures placed around the children's section.

2. Place a red and black Mickey Mouse on a white linoleum tile background tied in with other Walt Disney figures around the children's section.

3. Place a huge pink dragon on a blue linoleum tile background tied to other dragon figures around the children's section.

From these possibilities you can make your selection.

Utilizing this method, you can always come up with a number of possible solutions to any problem which will allow you to easily select the best possible one.

How to Raise Your Income to $100,000 a Year

Raising your income to $100,000 a year doesn't require a miracle; it simply requires the right kind of big money leverage. Look at it this way: no matter how little you're making right now, it's always possible, with a little effort, to add additional cash each year. If, for instance, you're making $8000 a year, you can easily add $800 with a part-time job or other part-time income producer. That's one level.

Once you begin a fortune-making business it's just as easy to add an additional 10 percent each year (or time period) to your overall gross.

If you're operating a mail order business making $50,000 a year, you might increase advertising or add an additional mailer which will raise your overall income by $5000. The trick is not to think in terms of $100,000 but in terms of small units that you can easily reach. Once you've reached that goal, add another 10 percent; then when you've consolidated that gain, add another 10 percent, and so on.

The main problem with this method is that you will reach critical points in your career where you will need additional energy, more money, or a change of direction to keep the momentum going.

For instance, if you're making $8000 a year and are saving toward a big capital nest egg, it's certainly possible to raise the money (utilizing all possible techniques) to launch your business. Once you raise the required cash, you then come to the end of one phase (raising money) and must now utilize additional energy to begin the next phase (a fortune-making business of your own). After that, your business will automatically increase on its own and then level off. At that point you will need additional energy (an extra wing to your building, a complete remodeling, a new store or something similar) to make any increase. The important point is to recognize what's happening, set a time for action, and then put that action into effect as we did in Chapter 4. This gets you off dead center and keeps you headed toward your big money goals. Once back on the money track, start making 10 percent increases as before.

Charley E., for instance, starting as a low-paid maintenance worker, decided early in his career to utilize the 10 percent method to propel himself to a big money income. At this point he was making $8000 a year. He increased this income 10 percent by raising and selling Christmas poinsettias. Charley simply grew the plants on his sun porch and then sold them for three dollars each at a local flea market.

Putting this amount in the bank along with an additional $6200 accumulated through savings, borrowing and moonlighting, Charley began to merchandise a family game which involved putting clues together to arrive at the solution to a crime.

By utilizing several jobbers and calling on department store buyers himself, he managed to gross $10,000 the first year. At this point he decided to initiate the 10 percent increase plan. The problem, of course, was how? Since he had a new product, however, Charley decided to try a news release to trade journals in his field (since these would reach thousands of retailers across the country.) He wrote the release, included a picture of the game and mailed it to 20 magazines directed to toy stores, discount stores, drug stores, department stores and similar businesses.

The result: $7200 in orders within six months, an increase far in excess of Charley's goal of 10 percent. With this accomplished, he started immediately on the next 10 percent increment. His sparkplug idea: To hire someone to demonstrate the game within each store and initiate sales right there. The first demonstration sold 50 games; each subsequent one sold 30 to 80, adding an additional $6000 profit within a five-month period.

For the next 10 percent increase, Charley decided to try a mail order gift brochure offering the game for Christmas, birthdays and other occasions. The result of an additional selected 10,000 mailing was $2000 profit. Over the next five years Charley boosted his income to well over $150,000 and then began to zero in on his first million—all the result of utilizing the 10 percent increment method.

Ten Magic Tips to Help You Mine the Full Potential of Your Wealth-Building Ideas

Ideas themselves are the raw material on which you will build your fortune throughout your career. Properly actionized, they will propel you to riches almost automatically. Most people, however, are content to simply begin, and then just take whatever comes along after that. Ideas, however, are like anything else—properly handled many have tremendous big money potential. Improperly or inefficiently handled, most will fail miserably.

Here are eight tips that will help you mine the full potential of your wealth building program.

> 1. *Give your ideas a priority:* Not every idea has the same degree of importance, yet frequently potential big money fortune builders simply draw up a list of ideas, and then proceed to put them into operation chronologically. To mine their real potential you must rate them as to just how much energy, money and effort you can economically invest in each.

Let's say, for instance, that you own a small retail business and have the following ideas listed in your notebook:

> 1. Change color of all signs to make them more striking.
>
> 2. Use a cartoon character logo for advertising.
>
> 3. Work up a direct mail flyer.
>
> 4. Turn off half the lights to save money.
>
> 5. Buy in larger quantities and drop-ship for bigger profits.

Now give these money-return priority by rating each on a scale of 0 to 10. In one particular case, Ralph H., a successful million-dollar-a-year retailer who started in business on a $500 shoestring, faced this problem. He rated sign color 1, the cartoon character 2, the direct mail flyer 8, the lights 1 and quantity discounts 3. This meant that from a money standpoint the flyer was critical, the quantity discounts second, the cartoon character third, and the lights and sign color least important,

Having about 40 hours of available time and a $2000 budget for these projects, Ralph decided to spend his time and money like this: direct mail flyer—28 hours, $1,400; the quantity discounts—5 hours; the cartoon logo—$300, 4 hours; the signs—$300, 4 hours, and the lights—2 hours.

The direct mail flyer returned $6200 in total profits; the quantity discounts saved an initial $3000 the first year, and the light program, $400. The color and cartoon character return could not be estimated directly, but overall business increased $75,000 that particular year.

2. *Try to give each idea a twist:* Every idea, when possible, should have something extra which makes it a better big money bet. The trick is to dream up the idea originally, then go over it again and add a different twist. Let's look at the ideas with which we were just working: changing the color of signs, a cartoon logo, a direct mail flyer, turning off the lights, buying in quantities or for drop shipment. First, what could be different about sign color? You should use polkadots instead of straight colors, or stripes, or maybe you could paint the signs a fluorescent orange. You could also utilize raised cutout letters, diagonal lettering or something similar—all variations on the basic idea. With the cartoon logo, you might make the logo extremely large, use reverse colors, or personalize an inanimate object such as a talking pen, a talking car or something similar. With the direct mail flyer you might utilize one sale object per page, use a coupon for giveaway items or print the entire flyer on jet-black paper.

As for turning out the lights, announce the fact (in your regular ads) that you are cutting down on lights to save energy; then pass the savings along to customers in the form of special prices. Make a big campaign out of the light turnoff by giving customers small penlights so they can find their way around your store (this is simply a novelty gimmick to get attention).

For the quantity discount or drop-ship discount, make up your own distributor container that can be packed easily, or ask for a drop shipment promising guaranteed quantities.

Sam T. managed to develop a $3000 investment into a $250,000 a year specialty pipe shop. His specialty was using novel "twists" to increase overall big money income. For instance, every Christmas, Sam hired a Santa Claus to stand out in front of his shop and say "Merry Christmas" to everyone who passed by—a good idea, but it needed an added twist. Since Sam's business was a pipe shop he decided to make up several hundred three-foot-long styrofoam pipes with "Merry Christmas from Sam's Pipe Shop" printed on the front. Santa Claus handed these out to all customers. The pipes themselves were so awkward, however, that customers couldn't put them away in a pocket or a purse. Therefore, for almost two weeks, several hundred people walked up and down the city streets carrying huge styrofoam pipes advertising Sam's pipe shop. The stunt not only generated tremendous publicity for Sam, but the entire city was talking about it for several months afterwards.

For another twist, Sam added a talking record with a new shelf display so customers could press a button and hear a 20-second recorded message on the history of the various pipes on display. This gimmick resulted in $700 in added income over a seven-day period.

Joseph Cossman too, a well-known mail order

millionaire, is famous for "extra idea" twists. Several years ago, Cossman's basic idea was to publicize a toy spud gun at the New York toy show. To this he added the following special twists:

He rented a room at the show and asked potato associations all across the country to send him enough potatoes to fill the room. He then sent news releases to every city newspaper desk, every human interest feature writer, economics editor, gossip columnist, and television and radio station in New York. He set up spud gun displays in stores around the convention center and handed out spud gun patrol honorary sheriff's badges to every person in attendance. Cossman also contacted an orphanage and offered them all the potatoes he collected if they would send him kids for a spud gun battle. In addition, he also had eight thousand pounds of potatoes dumped on the sidewalk in front of the hotel for a huge potato gun battle between the kids.

The result: (1) every newspaper and television station in New York City reported the promotion, (2) the spud gun battle made all the Sunday papers, (3) 50,000 pounds of potatoes arrived from potato associations across the country, (4) buyers swamped the Cossman suite where they found a room full of potatoes and models in potato sacks serving coffee, (5) buyers here were also invited to take a pot shot at a poster girl: those who hit the girl won three pounds of potatoes, and those who missed had to take six pounds, (6) Cossman oversold the spud gun by 400,000 units five days after the show opened.

When putting all ideas into action, then, try to add one novel twist on each routine idea and several on important ideas. For key ideas like the Cossman spud gun promotion, add enough twists to make the overall effect overwhelming.

To find good idea twists, simply search your imagination until you find angles or variations you feel are really different and engaging.

3. *Once you have created the idea in formal form, go through and look at it once more with money-colored glasses.*

It's a fact that direction can make a tremendous difference in an idea's big money potential. Focus on money and generally you can make that idea produce at maximum. Ignore money and, while the idea itself may work, it won't always succeed financially.

After you have conceived the idea then, go back over each one and review it with money in mind. Will this idea add to your overall money program? Will it attract attention and eventually produce a maximum amount of cash? If not, how can you maximize its money potential?

In relation to the sign idea discussed earlier in this chapter, for instance, signs of the same size generally produce about the same results. If you make the signs small for some items and large and important for others, the large signs tend to sell the most merchandise. This is a good example of how to make an idea produce just a little bit better by focusing on money considerations. Throughout your entire big money career you should handle each idea in a similar manner.

Tim R. was formerly a $7000-a-year railroad employee until he ran a $3000 investment into a million dollar a year fast food restaurant chain, utilized this method extensively to millionize every idea. One idea, for instance, was to print huge menus outside on the restaurant wall where people could see them before coming inside. The original idea Tim felt was a good one, but needed additional money orientation. He then picked out a steak dinner priced slightly above the medium order, marked it "house special" and gave it additional space on the menu. As a result, orders for this particular steak dinner picked up considerably, resulting in $1700 a month in increased dollar volume.

During the remainder of that year, Tim reviewed each idea to maximize its money potential, altering each one where necessary. The result: a good $25,000 overall income increase for that year, directly attributal to Tim's idea-money orientation.

4. *Put your idea in writing:* To really maximize your idea, put the entire idea in writing. This makes it more concrete and forces you to focus on all the details. Simply write down the idea at the top of a piece of paper, then make notations as to how you intend to implement it below. Some big money fortune builders maintain an idea file for all written ideas of this type so they can refer back at any time to make additional notations.

Ben Henderson, for instance, utilized this method throughout his entire career, starting as an $8000-a-year garage mechanic and ending as a millionaire, multiple parking lot owner. In one particular case, Ben was having trouble filling one of his parking lots during the week. During one of his idea sessions he decided to try to solve his problem by turning it into exclusively doctors' parking. Ben then sat down and put the entire plan in writing, underlining the important points: he intended to stress security; would shuttle doctors to and from their offices; issue monthly bills; offer the doctors such extra services as tuneups, gas fillups, tire replacements and similar extras—in other words, provide a special MD service. The result—the lot filled up one month later, bringing Ben an additional $8000 a month in added income.

The reason for his tremendous success, Ben decided, was that he had the idea written down so that it seemed more important. It also enabled him to visualize the items he needed to emphasize, and the written idea almost forced him to act where he might have been tempted to procrastinate otherwise.

5. *Review your idea immediately before you implement it:* Needs and conditions change constantly; therefore, you should take another look at your idea before you actually put it into use. Decide at this point if this really is the best possible idea you could come up with and if it will do the desired job effectively.

Bryan Mackenzie, a multimillionaire advertising executive who made a $300 investment into millions by becoming a television advertising expert, had for years simply put his ideas together and then rushed them into production.

With one, however—the idea of creating a gun display gimmick—he decided to make a quick review before putting it into action. In thinking it over, he decided that maybe an entire wall of guns, instead of a gun display, would attract more attention on TV. Bryan then made the change, produced the ad, and ran it for several weeks. The result: the ad outpulled anything he'd ever done, with customers coming into that particular store for several weeks afterwards just to see the wall of guns for themselves.

6. *Once you get your idea going, give it lots of publicity:* Without a doubt, you can increase the effectiveness of a good idea many times through publicity. After all, if no one knows anything about it, nothing will happen.

James E., a big money fortune builder who turned $1000 into a $500,000-a-year dog grooming empire, came up with an unusual idea motif: drapes and beautiful furnishings, poodle drawings on the walls, and similar improvements. Customers expressed approval and mentioned how nice the place looked, but business stayed about the same. At this point James decided to get some newspaper publicity. He called all the local newspapers and told them about the change. He then had several pictures taken, wrote up a news item on the subject and sent it to eight newspapers. As a result, four local newspapers ran pictures and two more picked up the news story. Several people came in to look for themselves. In addition, business picked up an additional $600 that particular month, all attributal to the added publicity.

In another case, Roger B., running the same kind of business, came up with several laborsaving ideas to clip dogs more quickly. He put the ideas into operation and publicized this fact in the local newspapers. Roger also sent mention of all these ideas to seven trade journals in his field. The newspaper material created some interest but little new business. The trade journal item, however, brought an offer of a $25,000 retainer from a manufacturer who needed advice on a similar operation he intended to put into effect, a result well worth the time and effort it took to create additional publicity.

If your idea is one that will attract retail trade, talk it up to everyone you see; then call the local newspapers or send out a news release to any papers you feel might have some interest. If your idea is something that might interest others in your business or profession, write it up as a news release for the trade magazines and send it off to any that might have an interest.

7. *Don't rely on the opinions of others:* In the last analysis, only you can decide whether or not to try any particular idea. Sometimes you'll find your

best ideas are the ones other people have discarded as useless.

Joseph Cossman, for instance, when considering the spud gun idea, sent letters to many people including his own representatives to see what they thought of the idea. Since the spud gun had been marketed and flopped, every last person advised against trying it again. Understanding, however, that he must rely on his own counsel, Cossman liked the item and decided to go ahead. As a result he eventually sold a million and a half spud guns before the kids finally lost interest.

It is fine to test your ideas on other people, but they will generally look at that idea with their own prejudices and knowledge. Because of this they frequently miss just what you are trying to do. You must, therefore, in the final analysis, make your own decision. If you feel something will work despite what others say, you must put yourself behind the idea and proceed as if you're going to have a real winner.

8. *Be curious about how others are using similar ideas:* Similar ideas others are using can actually add thousands to your original idea. Why? Because these ideas will often trigger angles or variations that can make you millions.

Skip MacK. is a Seattle restaurant owner who turned a $500 nest egg into a million-dollar restaurant empire. Skip constantly utilized the "similar idea" method in accumulating his fortune. What he wanted originally was a potato dicer that would produce fancy designs. While visiting a nearby city, he happened to eat dinner in a restaurant that presented lettuce and other vegetables diced into designs similar to those he had planned for the potatoes. This triggered an idea variation. Why not create designs for other foods including jello, pudding, ice cream, cranberry sauce and other foods?

On Halloween, for instance, Skip served ice cream in the form of a flat pumpkin. At Thanksgiving, the cranberry sauce took on the likeness of a turkey. For this additional treat, Skip charged ten cents extra per plate, resulting in $3000 in additional profits during the first year.

To utilize this method yourself, simply observe what other people are doing that's similar to your original problem, determine exactly how they achieved results, then try to add an additional twist or modify the idea to fit your own needs.

Get Your Big Money Ideas Moving Immediately

Time is always money; sometimes even a single day can be worth several million dollars.

Bryce B., for instance, who invented several kinds of devices to make the internal combustion engine operate more efficiently, was tempted to put off patenting his first idea because of the expense. He needed the money desperately, but decided to go ahead anyway. When the patent came through, Bryce discovered that someone else had come up with almost the same idea, but that Bryce had beaten him by three days. Within four months, several manufacturers made good offers, one of which he selected. Eventually, Bryce B. realized almost a million dollars from the idea—money he would have lost if he had waited even an additional month.

To make sure that you get every advantage possible, then, move on every idea at the first moment it becomes possible; procrastination or footdragging may well cost you big money.

Keep Looking For New Wealth Building Idea Sources

Ideas, as we've seen, are everywhere, yet you never know when you'll find just the one idea that will make you a million dollars. This means you should constantly stay on the alert for new idea sources. These sources might be books, magazines, certain TV shows, government pamphlets or newsletters.

One fortune builder, for instance, finds that the short times he spends glancing through *Popular Science, Popular Mechanics, Mechanix Illustrated* and other similar magazines often trigger ideas which can be modified for his own use to produce extra cash. One fortune builder who manufacturers gardening equipment often finds good money-making ideas in *Sunset* magazine; another constantly browses through sources like the *Whole Earth Catalog;* still another subscribes to a government list of new patents which frequently produces ideas he can modify.

For your own use, simply make a list of sources that seem especially productive for you and keep adding to that list whenever you discover something new that you think might prove useful.

POINTS TO CONSIDER

1. Ideas can multiply your fortune-building power many times.

2. Once you decide to try an idea, really commit yourself to it.

3. Look for big money idea possibilities everywhere. Jot down whatever you think you can use. Good places to look are: conversations, hobbies, homes and gardens, magazines and newspapers, businesses and professions.

4. Try to make all ideas take advantage of your natural abilities.

5. Try to see how your idea fits into the big picture and the future course of your own business.

6. Utilize a big money think period scheduled for the same time each week.

7. Increase your big money wealth by giving ideas a
priority, by adding a new twist to each, by thinking about each idea in terms of money, by putting
the major ideas in writing, by publicizing major
ideas, by reviewing the idea before putting it in
use, by making the final decision yourself, by
examining similar ideas, by getting your money
ideas moving immediately and by staying on the
alert for new idea sources.

10

How to Throw Off
the Chains of Convention
and Make Money Fast

Conventional methods often work well as basic building blocks for accumulating wealth, but sometimes you can zoom to your big money goals much faster by simply ignoring convention.

Luther R., for instance, was a $7200-a-year high school custodian until he parlayed his model railroad hobby into a $200,000-a-year business. He ran into a real problem as he began to put his business together, however.

During the first year, Luther utilized a back room of his house as a workshop and, sparked by the growing interest in railroad nostalgia, sold $50,000 worth of kits, parts and other equipment.

At that point he decided to build a small store on a piece of land that he had owned for the past ten years. First he called several contractors and asked for bids on the building. The lowest was about $27,000. Next he priced the material at a local lumberyard. This totaled about $7400, still too much for his resources. Luther then reasoned that if he intended to go ahead he must come up with an unconventional method to get the job done. Salvaging lumber from a torn-down building would be unconventional; so would cutting the timber himself and then hauling it to a mill. Looking around, Luther discovered a contractor tearing down an old bridge about seven miles outside of town. Since the contractor intended to burn the timber, he gave Luther permission to haul the lumber away free. Luther then rented a flat bed truck for $45 and hauled the large beams to his construction site. He obtained siding from a fallen down barn.

When finished, the building looked smartly rustic, probably a more interesting structure for this particular business than Luther R. could have hired a contractor to build, and the total cost came to less than $2000. Spurred by the imaginative setting and complete railroad display Luther erected, business jumped to a gross of well over $100,000 the first year—all the result of using an unconventional shortcut.

Besides this kind of a building shortcut, there are dozens of others you can take that will make you rich: shortcutting paperwork, going around channels, utilizing unconventional materials, improvising everywhere to shortcut expense and many more.

How To Make Unconventionality Pay Off Big

To maximize your fortune, always consider the unconventional method first, then decide what you can do to turn that method into a gold mine at that particular moment.

Walt B., for instance, was a $12,000-a-year railroad worker with a part-time job selling steel. For a long time he sold conventionally through purchasing agents at various companies. Trying to decide how to maximize his earnings, Walt carefully considered all the conventional ways of increasing business. These consisted of contacting more purchasing agents every day, convincing each company to place larger steel orders and so forth. He also decided to try some unconventional routes. Company presidents, he reasoned, could swing big orders and tie up large contracts—so he put together a package plan of special services. Walt would promise one-day delivery; companies could return unused inventory; materials would come specially packed; inventory and reordering would be automatic, and discounts would go from five to 15 percent depending on volume. All of this created a special advantage for any customer ordering on a package plan basis.

Walt then made an appointment with one company president and presented the complete package of services along with the advantages. The first company president turned him down, but the second decided to give it a try, resulting in an immediate $500,000 increase in business—all because Walt had the nerve to try a big money unconventional approach. Today Walt B. has a million-dollar-a-year structural steel business.

The trick, then, is to consider all conventional methods first. Next let your imagination run wild and list all the unconventional methods you can think of. Don't try to rush this process—work on it for three or four days. At the end of this time, ask yourself if you've discovered a short cut or two that will pay off big. Usually the more unconventional the idea, the bigger the gamble, but since many provide excellent short cuts, give them a try if they seem at all plausible. Simply weigh what you have to loose against what you have to gain and then make your decision.

How To Be Far Out For Extra Cash

You can, without a doubt, make big money utilizing conventional methods. But you can also sometimes push your business ahead spectacularly and immediately by looking at your particular business in way-out ways.

Joseph Cossman, the mail order genius, for instance, sold necklaces by mail at one time. These sold reasonably well, but by the end of one particular Christmas season Cossman found himself stuck with a 500-necklace surplus. After thinking it over, Cossman couldn't think of any real way to sell this surplus at a reasonable profit. About that time, however, hypnotism had become a fad and Cossman enrolled in a course out of curiosity. The first night the instructor told them that to induce a hypnotic state you needed a "point of fixation." From that moment on Cossman began thinking "way out." Each of those 5000 necklaces, he realize, contained seven stones, resulting in 35,000 points of fixation!

Cossman rushed the teacher to a recording studio and made a self-hypnosis record. After that he created a mail order package consisting of a hypnotic course on a long-playing record, a hypnotic stone (a gemstone from the necklace) and an instruction booklet. Cossman immediately sold every last necklace in stock and then went on to sell well over one hundred thousand hypnotic courses—a spectacular unconventional success.

As a matter of fact, there isn't any type of fortune-making business that you can't market unconventionally. You can, for instance, link a secretarial service with the phone and type sermons for ministers dictated over the phone. You can employ a typist and one of the new word-processing machines in a complete inventory system for small business.

A roadside fruit and vegetable business could serve well as a mail order outlet for native fruit gifts. A telephone answering service might well be turned into a specialized phone sales business. Miniature trains, for instance, might be sold as lamp decorations, as a base for clocks, or as a frame around pictures. The rule is to look at what you're now doing. Give your imagination full reign, then try to link your final product to a different use.

Think Like a Child To Make an Extra Million

Frequently we tie ourselves down so tightly to the conventional routine way of doing things that we overlook the simpler, more direct methods that will make us an immediate million. Children never have this problem. They always see simply and directly, seldom mixing the rules of society or practicality with their final goals.

In a contest sponsored by Eaton Corporation, children were encouraged to develop ideas to solve many of today's problems, regardless of the practicality of their ideas. A few of the ideas the children came up with were: an invention that makes inventions (just push a button and out comes all sorts of inventions); a push-button house where the roof lifts up to let in the sun; a truckcopter, a cross between a helicopter and a truck that moves tons of goods through the sky at 200 miles an hour; a bike burglar detector; a transmitter sends the burglar's picture directly to a satelite, then back to the child's bedroom; a car balanced on springs that won't bump into other cars (any bump springs it off the highway high above other cars). All are great ideas which ignore the practical problems involved. We adults, of course, keep hemming ourselves in by practicalities, but sometimes it's possible to make a fortune by skipping the practical details until much later.

Consider, for instance, the fortune builder who turned a $100 deposit into over a million dollars in real estate. Roger F. had a chance to buy a single family house for $2000. The catch was that the house had to be moved 5 miles to his own lot. The cost quotes from conventional movers ran much too high, so Roger decided to go back to basics and think "like a child". He sat down and started listing some simple straightforward "house moving" ideas: pick it up with a helicopter; move it with a balloon; flood the street and float the house away; cut it into sections with a saw, then haul it away in a truck; make it disappear, then reappear at the site.

After dreaming them up, Roger took each of the wild far-out methods and tried to make them practical. The weight of a house was too much for a helicopter or a balloon. Flooding the street was out of the question. He could, however, cut the house into sections. As a matter of fact, three men with a chain saw could do the job within three or four hours. The sections then could be flown directly to the lot by helicopter. The total cost was $3000. Put back together, the house brought Roger well over $28,000—a clear profit after all deductions of $21,000—all a result of thinking like a small child and completely ignoring the practical at first, then turning the impractical into a practical application as a final step.

How To Use The "What If" Method To Extra Riches

In addition to thinking like a child, you'll find the "what if" method extremely effective in opening the door to automatic big money. The trick again is to ignore convention and ask yourself "what if . . ."

In the house example, for instance, you could have said, "What if I rent a pump, hook into the river and create a lake. I can then float the house away, or what if I cut the house into sections, then move each section with a helicopter, or what if I rent a giant truck, or an airship, or a crane?" Just keep on going until the answer comes easily and automatically.

Richard T., for instance, a Denver millionaire who boosted $300 in borrowed and saved capital into an ice skating rink fortune, utilized the "what if" method throughout his entire career.

In the beginning Richard simply sat down and said "What if I bought an ice rink . . . what if I paid for it from the sale of five apartment houses . . . what if I buy the apartment houses one by one . . . what if I buy the first apartment house by selling remodeled houses at a profit . . . what if I start with one old run-down house and go from there?"

Richard then put the "what if" plan into action utilizing the $300 as a down payment. At the end of two years he owned five apartment houses; by the end of three years he had accumulated almost two million dollars and had begun to construct his first ice skating rink.

In utilizing the "what if" method you'll find it easier to start with the goal and work backwards. Come up with four or five alternates, then select the method from these that seems to fit your money-making plans best.

How To Unblock Your Path To A Big Money Fortune

The basic big money rule you must remember is that there is money lying around everywhere. Often, however, many would-be fortune builders miss many opportunities because they're hemmed in by standard practices and their own straight-jacketed thinking. Sometimes, to unblock your path, it's best to simply go your own way, ignoring rules, regulations, and all other conventional problems.

You should closely examine every standard business practice. Here are a few you can easily short-cut for big money savings: job bidding, conventional credit forms, employee holidays, standard business hours, standard work weeks, utilizing the mail for letters and packages. All of these are conventional practices that we take for granted. Sometimes, however, it's possible to tap a gold mine by ignoring every one of these practices.

Go back and list all conventional methods that currently affect your business including forms, money paid out, conventional ordering methods, and transportation—then see if you can twist these around to either save money or increase volume.

Creditors, for instance, generally expect you to pay within 60 days. What if, instead, you put them off, banked this money for four months and utilized the interest in your own business? That's a gain you'd never make by following standard business practices.

Smart money fortune builders make millions every year by simply playing by a different set of "rules" than their competitors. Business generally follows a standard routine that makes things easier. Sometimes, however, it's absolutely necessary to temporarily short-cut conventional practice if you expect to make really big money.

Gene B., for instance, a former $10,000-a-year bus driver who started a Miami building materials business, made it a practice to take advantage of smart money short-cuts that his competitors ignored. Other city stores, Bickford realized, utilized untrained clerks who had little building knowledge. In addition, they wouldn't hire anyone over 65.

Gene decided people over 65 represented a potential gold mine. After all, a tremendous number knew the painting, building, electrical work, plumbing and other trades inside out, and could give customers really expert advice. After thinking it over Gene decided to give them a try.

For his paint department he hired two retired painters, for the plumbing department a retired plumber who had handled every conceivable kind of job. There wasn't anything a home-owner could do that Gene didn't have an expert to cover, all of them people who were delighted to share their many years of experience. Within ten months, as a result, Gene had quadru-pled his volume to almost $800,000 a year.

In another case "Mac" McL., who began developing crystal gemstones utilized by the superconductor and laser industry, was told by his competitors that it was impossible to start that kind of business for anything under $100,000 in capital. In addition, he was told that no one could possible sell an over-$1000 item by direct mail.

Ignoring this conventional thought, Mac raised $20,000 and started in business. He also used direct mail extensively. "My wife," Mac explained, "was put in charge of this, and she didn't know you couldn't sell a $1000 item by direct mail." As a result, sales zoomed immediately to several hundred thousand dollars a year.

The rule: question every conventional business practice. Ask yourself if there is any way of modifying the practice to acquire a real advantage. If the answer is yes, decide just how you intend to go about it, then put your plan into action immediately.

How To Make Selfishness Your Big Money Bonanza

A little practical "selfishness," or self-interest, is undoubt-edly one of the best tools available for adding extra big money cash to any business deal. In a deal we generally become so concerned about being "fair" to the other person that we lose the big money advantages that do come our way. Now is the time, however, to close this "selfishness gap" and keep any and all unexpected cash for yourself.

Sam E., for instance, in the process of remodeling a house

he had purchased for $3000 down, had ordered lumber from a local firm at an agreed-upon price. When the order arrived, the firm billed him for an extra $250. On inquiry, the firm told Sam that the salesman had made a mistake originally, but if he insisted they would honor the original price. This confronted Sam with a decision. He could be "fair" and pay the additional $250 or he could be selfish and utilize the money for himself in other ways. Sam's first inclination was to let the whole thing ride, but then he realized he was in the business of creating his own fortune, not theirs, and this $250 could well be a stepping stone that would push him that much further along.

This time Sam decided to be selfish and have the $250 returned. Putting this aside with an additional $750, he invested in an old house which, when remodeled, brought an additional $11,000 profit—a profit Sam would have passed up if he had not utilized the "be selfish" principle at that particular moment.

When driving toward your big money goals, then, selfishness is one of the best big money tools you have. If properly used, it can turn marginal deals into really profitable ones.

The rule is: put yourself first. If Sam, for instance, had placed the other fellow first he would have thrown away $250 in fortune-building cash. Always ask yourself: "What's best for me?" When the step you're about to take is not to your advantage, stop right there, withdraw and go in a different direction.

How To Turn Time Restrictions Into Your Big Money Pathway

Time is a huge obstacle for each and every one of us. After all, we just have so much time available and this, unfortunately, limits the number of big money projects we can undertake. Once started on your fortune building career, big money opportunities and ideas will multiply almost astronomically. Many will look so good that you just can't wait to jump in. The big problem is, of course, that every idea takes time to develop and you just can't possibly tackle them all.

In addition, you as an individual have just so much energy available. If you spend your time and energy on a number of projects you will scatter the results, but if you concentrate all energy and time on one project and relate everything you do to that project, then your force and energy will multiply itself many times.

Bob B., for instance, a big money fortune builder who turned a $3000 investment in an old Western farm into a multimillion dollar ski resort fortune, found himself three years behind after scattering both his time and energy to such a point that he had almost come to a standstill. First Bob bought the farm and began to repair the big rambling farmhouse. He then began to build his own home in a city some distance away. He next invested in a small dry cleaning establishment which he undertook to manage. He also started cutting firewood and selling it to people around the city. Each of these projects, while good, utilized time and didn't build on one another. As a result, by the end of the year all of his projects were just getting started. The old farm building was in the beginning stages of being remodeled. He had half completed his own home. The dry cleaning plant needed a complete reorganization, and he had received over 300 firewood orders but had managed to fill only five.

Bob then took stock and decided he must concentrate his time and energy on one basic project at a time. His first priority, he decided, must be the old farm house. He concentrated first on the remodeling and finished the project within four months. After that he borrowed money and added a skating rink, started a publicity campaign, bought a sleigh and began building a restaurant in one wing of the old farmhouse. The result: the property value increased $70,000 the first year and attracted 300 guests who payed a total of $125,000.

By the third year Bob had dozens of investors clamoring to finance the ski lifts and other improvements. After that the resort really took off until eventually it boasted five chair lifts, a ski shop, three restaurants, a larger lodge, several dormitories and many additional features.

At this point, Bob had become a millionaire several times over, all because he had learned to concentrate his energy within the available time to build toward a common goal.

There are many ways to make these principles work for you:

1. *Establish long-term goals.*

Bob, for instance after taking stock, set as his main goal "to make the ski resort return $2 million a year within four years." This larger goal, of course, automatically produced smaller ones. Bob sat down and established intermediate goals of $100,000 the first year, $750,000 the second, $1,250,000 the third and $2,000,000 the fourth. He then sat down and worked out exactly what he had to do to make this kind of money. After that he established projects that would lead directly to these goals.

2. *Plan what you have to do.*

After setting goals it is absolutely essential to plan how you intend to reach these goals. This will cut down gear-spinning time. Try to decide on the necessary steps. If, for instance, you plan to renovate a house, simply list what you intend to do: fix steps, repaint rooms, repair plumbing, paint the outside of house, and anything else. This type of planning applies to almost any kind of money goal which you have set for yourself.

3. *Concentrate on money only.*

In reaching goals concentrate only on the steps that will return immediate big money results. If, for instance, you consider adding an extra room to a house before selling it, think money. Estimate what the house would bring without the room;

then estimate the increase in value due to the room addition. After that decide if the project is worth the effort and if it will return a reasonable profit for the time involved. If not, don't begin the project; instead, utilize that time for tasks that will return a greater profit.

How "Not Keeping Up With The Joneses" Can Make You Rich

The American dream of fancy cars, fashionable clothes, big houses, luxury gadgets and keeping up with others (especially during the early fortune-building years) often works as a trap to keep you from reaching your big money goals in the shortest possible time.

Douglas H., for instance, a former telephone company employee who began a small rapid-print business on a $1600 nest egg, found himself grossing almost $85,000 a year by the end of the second year. Doug had at this point, acquired some well-to-do friends who drove fancy cars, belonged to an exclusive country club and owned large houses on a nearby lake. Instead of simply acknowledging these friendships and keeping to his own timetable, Doug tried to impress these "fancy" friends. He scrounged every last penny from his business, mortgaged it heavily and built himself a huge house in a fashionable section of town. Up to this point his business had expanded rapidly because he had plowed back all his profits. Suddenly growth stopped, business stagnated, and within a year Doug filed for bankruptcy when he couldn't meet the payments on a business loan.

Alex McG., on the other hand, handled a similar situation differently. Alex was a former Los Angeles warehouse worker who turned a $300 investment into a five-million-dollar chain of curbside photoshops. He also found himself meeting well-to-do friends within the first years of business success, but decided that instead of trying to keep up with his new friends, he'd rather invest any profits or extra cash in his own business. As a result, Alex remained in his $16,000 house, drove his older car a few more years and kept his life style about the same. By the end of the year he had accumulated a $25,000 business nest egg which he plowed into expansion instead of personal living expenses. The second year he added another $40,000 from the same source. This was obviously money that would have been lost if Alex had tried to keep up with his rich friends. Because of this extra expansion cash, Alex added three locations the first year and ten the second. Eventually he established a 25-chain that became a $9-million-a-year gold mine.

It is important, then, not to take expansion cash simply to better your own life style. Until your business has become established, resist trying to keep up with friends and acquaintances and plow that money back into your own fortune-making business. After your business has become really successful you can live in any style you like, without cutting down on your big money expansion possibilities.

Ignore Money Limitations To Strike It Rich

Believe it or not, not having enough money is a state of mind. Money itself can't actually hold you back; it's how you feel about money that acts as a deterrent. If, for instance, you believe you can't raise money for a project, then you probably can't. If, however, you know deep down that you'll acquire all the money you need when you need it, you will almost always find the cash somehow. The secret is to put so much mental pressure on yourself that you must come up with the money.

Timothy L., for instance, a former Chicago library worker who turned a $50 investment into a $600,000-a-year novelty business, constantly utilized the principle of ignoring cash limitations to create his own fortune. Timothy manufactured (in a spare bedroom) clever wall sayings which he sold by mail. At the end of the first year he had outgrown the bedroom and desperately needed to move into large quarters. In addition, he needed to start handling other marketing operations. Unfortunately, this required an additional $10,000 which Timothy L.

simply didn't have. Ignoring this, however, he decided to simply go ahead and act. First he applied for a loan with the Small Business Administration; then he signed a contract for a small shop, purchased $4000 worth of materials and took on an additional $4000 in labor commitments. At this point, Timothy had no possible way to meet any of these obligations. Three weeks before he had to lay out the cash, the Small Business Administration turned him down for a loan. He now had nowhere to go; however, he just kept telling everyone who'd listen about his problem and applying for loans everywhere. Two days before the first due date, Timothy attended a party where (in his usual manner) he mentioned his need for money. The next day the phone rang. The voice on the other end told Timothy that this person had attended the party, had money to invest, and would like to discuss it with him. The result; Timothy got the loan and the expansion went ahead on schedule, earning him an estimated $500,000 over the next 12 months. During the next three years, Timothy repeated this procedure several times. It was at this point that he realized that as long as he believed in himself and acted as if he couldn't lose, the money would somehow always materialize.

The trick in using this method is to make a commitment, sign a contract, buy a building—do anything that will put you under pressure to come up with the money you need—then start doing everything possible to help yourself. The intensity and need will soon take over and no matter what the odds, the money, generally, will always show up.

Pursue Profits Everywhere

Always limit profits to conventional money-making sources—Right? Wrong! Not only should profits come in conventional ways but, if you're really dedicated to fortune making, you must take in profits everywhere. This again necessitates thinking in far-out, outlandish ways.

Suppose, for instance, you've established a landscape service and you're sent by a client to a distant city (on expenses) to put in several large trees. Now, of course, you will bill for the actual labor involved and the plants themselves, but what about the additional expenses? Say you flew to a distant city, shipped the plants by air freight, rented a truck and made several phone calls. These items create additional expenses which you must cover. If, however, you bill (as is traditional) for the dollar amount of these expenses, you will simply be turning dollars. In addition, these expense items are just as much a part of your inventory as the plants themselves and should be so considered when figuring profit.

If the truck rental comes to $40, add enough to return a 20 percent profit (in this case, $10, for a $50 billing). You could bill $8 worth of phone calls at $10, a $24 plane ticket at $32. The principle is that any time you spend money in advance, you are entitled to a fair profit from that time and money. This is not the conventional way of looking at profit— but it is essential if you intend to maximize your wealth-building potential.

Gregg B., is a Kansas City fortune builder who turned a $1000 down payment into a $10 million rental-real estate fortune. Gregg charged families renting his homes and apartments, the first and last months' rent in advance, plus a $100 security deposit. This money he invested for a minimum 10 percent return. In addition, he offered renters a decorating service, supplying wallpaper and other decorating materials with which renters could individualize their homes, all at a 35 percent profit. Gregg also provided for mothers a baby sitting service which returned a good fee. Overall Gregg estimates that he adds an additional $10,000 a year by thinking of profits in terms of the total possible profit picture rather than from just the conventional rental income source.

Simply look at your own operation and ask yourself what you do that could be tapped for additional profit. For instance, do you pay out expense money on which you could tag an additional profit? What other items or services could you add to your primary profit picture? Plug these loopholes immediately and start taking profits in every possible area.

POINTS TO REMEMBER

1. Conventional methods often limit your profit. When necessary, approach profit making in the simplest, most direct way possible.

2. Try looking at what you're doing in different ways. Frequently your product or service can bring more profit when utilized for a different market or use.

3. Adults tend to think in conventional roundabout ways. Whenever possible (no matter how impractical it seems at the moment), try thinking in a straight line like a child.

4. When stuck, try utilizing the "what-if" techniques to maximize profits.

5. Unblock your path to big money by ignoring conventional methods and rules.

6. Always "think selfish" to make really big money.

7. Make time work for you by establishing long-term goals and by getting rid of any time expenditure that does not advance these goals.

8. Think of everything in terms of money.

9. Do not let yourself get caught in the "keeping up with the Joneses" trap.

10. Try to make a profit out of all the unconventional facets of your operation.

11

Nine Money Management Short-Cuts That Will Make You Rich

In creating your big money fortune it's important to utilize every possible method that will speed you along almost automatically to real riches. In every endeavor you'll find standard methods that will get the job done adequately, and also short-cuts that will speed you along toward your goals without sacrificing quality. Every task today requires so much time and energy that it is vitally important to always look for short-cuts that will allow you to turn saved time and energy into still more big money projects. In that way you will maximize the effect of all your efforts. In mapping out any fortune-building plan there are nine basic money management short-cuts that will help give your big money career a real push. Consider these:

1. *See the Whole Big Money Picture.*

In planning any project it's important to see the entire picture first. Simply sit down and think it out from one end to the other to decide how all the different parts fit together properly. This will save you much extra time and effort.

If you've decided to establish a small restaurant, for instance, the entire picture will look something like this: getting the idea, finding the financing, obtaining the building, physically putting the restaurant together and beginning business.

Anthony F., a retired $8000-a-year telephone company employee, opened a restaurant. In the beginning, he concentrated on one step at a time, not bothering to coordinate the steps themselves. Anthony decided, for instance, that he needed exactly $6000 to launch the business. He then took his $3000 savings, borrowed $3000, and began to remodel a building to meet his requirements. Several weeks afterwards, however, he realized costs would exceed his estimates by at least $6000. He then had to go back and raise the extra money, creating a four-month opening delay.

In addition, Anthony had room in the restaurant for about 85 people, but parking spaces for only 55 (considering the average number in the car). As a result he had to quickly remodel the parking lot, disrupting his entire schedule and adding to overall cost.

On opening his next restaurant, however, Anthony established the restaurant size first, considered the motif and decor, and then planned the parking to match the restaurant capacity. He then estimated the cost and added a 50 percent fudge factor. That way he waited to launch the new venture until he had located enough cash to do the job right. As a result, no major loopholes developed when the restaurant opened, and it became a huge success almost immediately, enabling Anthony to move another step up the fortune ladder.

To see the big money picture, sit down and put together an overall idea of what you're going to do. List the details then try to see how these fit together. After that, try to plan accordingly. You will, of course, make mistakes, but seeing the big money picture in the first place will, overall, return many thousands of dollars over the life of your fortune-building career.

2. *Check Out Several Possibilities At One Time*

Time always means money; therefore, you must quickly check as many possibilities as you can. James R. created a million-dollar fortune in mail order novelties. Once he decided to manufacture and market a bubble pipe that initial tests indicated the kids would really love. Production capacity, however, wouldn't come anywhere close to filling the expected volume of orders. James then contacted tool and die makers to see about the possibilities of making additional sets of tooling. He worked up a proposal to rent a building, and manufacture the pipes himself. At the same time he contacted several manufacturers and suppliers to see about the possibility of contracting out the manufacturing to a number of plants. He also explored the possibility of having one firm handle the whole procedure from manufacturing through sales for a percentage of the profits.

By establishing his own manufacturing plant, James estimated he could lower the costs to about nine cents a pipe; by contracting out the manufacturing and handling the marketing himself, 11 cents. The 22-cent cost, however, required no supervision, thus freeing James to handle other projects.

By checking out all these possibilities at once, James made a quick evaluation, then moved the project into production almost immediately, creating a $100,000-plus quick money profit within three months.

The trick is to simply sit down and decide what the possibilities are. Check everything at the same time. Write for information, call, or do whatever you have to do. When finished, sit down and evaluate each option, picking the one that fits your needs best.

3. *Make Quick Money Decisions*

Really successful big money fortune builders always apply this formula: Make decisions quickly, then deliberate a long time before changing that decision. There is an extremely good reason for this. It takes a great deal of energy to worry about whether or not you are making the right decision. In many cases that time spent waivering creates a tension that wastes energy. It would be far better to get all the information together, go over it two or three times, and then decide quickly. In this way you can put saved time and energy into other projects.

Suprisingly, you will often find that all decisions are more or less right and once you make one you will then proceed in a direction that will automatically lead to your goal. The basic ingredient of all fortune building is movement: movement—any movement—will bring you to your goal eventually. Inaction, however, will keep you from ever reaching your objective.

Suppose, for instance, you are in the mail order business and are deliberating whether to sell a bird house, a giant pen or a cuckoo clock. In general, any product you pick after a preliminary market study will produce some results. In addition, you can always market the other products later. The same principle applies to almost everything you do throughout your fortune-building career.

Bottomly McG. constantly utilized this principle in all his fortune-building operations. Bottomly had several years before begun photographing high school rodeo performers and selling the prints to performers right at the rodeo. He strongly believed in simply making a decision, right or wrong, and then going on from there. When, for instance, he needed a portable photo lab, his choices were: to buy a motor home, to build an inexpensive trailer, or to buy a used camper. In each case the space would have to be fully equipped as a laboratory.

Since Bottomly was short of cash, he made an immediate decision to spend $200 to build his own trailer. After putting the trailer together he used it as a photo lab for a year, creating an estimated $42,000 profit. At the end of that time he sold the trailer for $600 and then used some of his profits to buy a motor home which he equipped as a super photo lab.

By making a quick decision, he got his operation going quickly on the available cash, saved for a year the interest on a motor home loan, and made a profit he otherwise would have lost.

Some alternatives are so opposed, of course, that one will bring success and the other disaster, but generally most decisions are gradations of each other. Any decision you make, therefore, will be at the very least partially successful. In the meantime you are in action on the way to where you really want to go.

4. *Never Pay The Asking Price*

Tom H. is a smart money millionaire who has built a $50 investment into a several million-dollar-a-year high performance auto parts distributorship. Tom always makes a point of never paying the asking price for anything. He feels that if he buys just $100,000 worth of materials a year and can save two percent on each item that he can then pocket a good $2000 which he can then use in other fortune-building activities.

Tom, himself, utilizes a definite formula for this. First of all, he always obtains bids from at least three suppliers. He then begins with the highest and tries to convince him to reduce the bid slightly. If that suppliers offers to reduce the price by, say, $1000, Tom goes to the second supplier and asks if he'll match or better that offer. With these two bids, he goes next to the lowest bidder and repeats the procedure. Sometimes the third supplier won't reduce his bid at all, but frequently Tom receives a price break of some kind, a differential which, over a period of years, adds up to a substantial amount that can be ploughed back to make still more money.

When dealing with small amounts, of course, you generally won't bother with bids, but should always ask for a discount. Remember, unless you ask, you'll never save a penny, yet it's important to shortcut everywhere possible, reinvesting these savings in your own fortune building for even greater growth.

5. *Always Utilize The Fewest Possible Steps*

Every task you undertake in the course of your fortune building consists of a series of individual steps which you must perform. Something as simple as placing an ad, for instance, consists of at least eight steps. You must decide what the ad will say, put the ad in writing, call or send it in, and so forth. Each of these steps takes a certain amount of time which could be used in other ways to create more big money fortune, provided you could reduce the necessary steps. With the ad, for instance, if you are trying to sell a house, instead of dreaming up a new ad, you might find a similar one in the classified section that will work for you. All you need to do is substitute your own address and phone number and it's ready to go. A procedure like this can save as much as 30 minutes. Multiply this by all the tasks you perform and you can see what a tremendous amount of time it's possible to save.

Generally, experienced fortune builders do this by going through (in their own minds at least) three ways of handling each task. They enumerate the number of steps required for each task and then pick the method that requires the least time. With practice you'll find it's possible to go through this procedure in your own mind within a few seconds.

Ralph H. was a $7000-a-year Los Angeles retail clerk until he parlayed a $300 investment into a fortune in candles. Ralph always utilizes this method in handling required tasks. He has been at this so long that he goes through the whole procedure automatically.

If he wants to redesign a shop, for instance, he reviews several methods, for example: handling all the details himself, hiring someone to do the design, hiring someone to both design and remodel. He then picks the one that saves the most time, effort and money and then puts that plan into action immediately.

Over the years, Ralph estimates he saves at least $15,000 a year, all by trying to do a task in the fewest number of steps possible.

To utilize this method effectively, look at every task and decide what steps you will need to take, then repeat the procedure with two alternative methods, trying to find methods that will require less work. Select the one that seems best, then try to combine and eliminate steps without reducing results. Finally, put the revised plan into action.

6. *Make Impatience Your Billion-Dollar Secret*

Nothing slows you down quite like drifting. When you simply let things happen without urgency, details tend to remain undone and progress often grinds to a complete halt. You can speed up any big money activity automatically by creating impatience.

Suppose, for instance, that you're in the process of preparing a house for rent and one of the subcontractors doesn't arrive to complete the electrical repairs. You can drift and simply wait until he shows up or you can bring impatience into play, get worked up about the slowdown, then call and put on pressure until you receive some action.

As another example, suppose the city refuses to issue a sign permit. You can use your impatience to call city officials, write letters, and keep the pressure on until you get action. Impatience is a tool that you can use to speed progress and get action when all else fails.

Van H. always uses impatience this way. Van was formerly a low-paid government worker who turned a small $500 down payment into a $10-million-dollar office rental fortune. Van says he makes use of impatience to keep his business going and to put over deals that he couldn't move any other way. He was at one time, for instance, in the process of trying to build a small office complex. When the seller began to drag his feet and tried to back out, Van became tremendously impatient and began putting on the pressure. First Van called the seller and asked that he close the deal immediatley. Next he called the man's lawyer. After that he talked to the seller's wife explaining what her husband would lose if the deal didn't go through. That did it. The seller showed up at Van's office and signed the papers just two hours after Van started his "get-impatient" campaign.

In using impatience as your own billion-dollar tool, simply mull the problem over until you're itching to get the project going; then turn it over and over in your mind demanding action until you've worked yourself up to the point where it has almost become an obsession. At this point impatience itself will take over and literally propel you into action automatically.

7. *Let Your Subconscious Make The Tough Money Decisions*

We have, of course, known how to utilize the

power of the subconscious mind for years. Napoleon Hill, in his book *Think and Grow Rich* (written in the 1920s), stresses the importance of utilizing the subconscious mind in all wealth-building programs. Recent research at leading universities shows that not only does the subconscious have the ability to solve problems but can achieve almost miraculous results.

Recent theories postulate that the subconscious is a very complicated computer—that once given a problem, it concentrates on that problem intently until it comes up with an answer. Put enough pressure on the computer (by emotionalizing the problem) and it will put you in touch with circumstances that will automatically solve the problem.

Ben Z., for instance, who turned a $70 investment into a concrete building block fortune, always turned to the subconscious to solve his more difficult problems.

Generally Ben would mull the problem over for a day or two, then consciously tell himself that he was turning the problem over to his subconscious mind and would like a solution. In one case, he simply couldn't come up with the $10,000 needed for a workman's compensation payment to keep the plant from being shut down. Ben turned the problem over to his subconscious and waited. The next day a few ideas began to filter through: he could go back to his banker and ask if he knew of private investors who might want to invest in Ben's type of enterprise; he could run a classified ad in business opportunities section looking for investors; he could talk to everyone he knew about investing.

He immediately started following up on these ideas. Surprisingly, the banker said he knew of a local car dealer who might want to invest a few thousand dollars. Ben immediately went to see the car dealer and made a deal within half an hour. Three months later the factory landed a five-million-dollar contract and within three years was grossing well over $10 million a year.

Here is how one million-dollar fortune builder utilizes his subconscious mind to solve problems. First he goes to a quiet spot and puts the problem he's trying to solve into his own words. For instance he might say, "I'm trying to find $10,000," or "I need to figure out how to repair a processing machine without buying a new part," or whatever. He states at this time what he thinks he can do; then he repeats this two or three times a day for several days until it becomes extremely important. He tries to emotionalize this thought as much as possible, becoming vitally concerned with solving the problem.

After three or four days, he stops this process and says, "I know I'll find the solution soon. Now I'll just wait for it to happen." If nothing happens within a few days he then repeats the process. Using this method, the solution generally appears to him within a few days, and he is then able to work his way out of the problem.

8. Keep Your Outgo Small

Keeping your outgo small is especially important in the beginning of your fortune-building career. This lets you utilize money for expansion immediately and leads you on to your goal that much faster.

Wright C., for instance, a former high school teacher, began a small bookstore on a $3000 nest egg in a small college town. The store did fairly well right from the beginning and began to create a surplus after the second year.

Wright had waited all his life for money and immediately bought a large car, moved into a luxury house, hired an interior decorator to spruce up the store, installed a huge sign, bought two delivery trucks, and added some new luxurious store fixtures.

These expenditures, however, really strapped Wright and prevented him from adding additional inventory. He was unable to order the needed new books and found he no longer had what customers wanted. Volume also declined a good $8000 over the second year's income.

Sim T., on the other hand began his book business with almost the same dollar capital. Again, Sim did well right from the beginning and started creating a surplus profit after the second year. Instead of increasing expenses, Sim put all surplus back in the business. He began creating additional departments and stocking specialty interests that people in the area requested. By the end of three years, the inventory grew from $8000 to over $45,000 and volume increased from a bare $25,000 to over $145,000 a year.

This happened because Sim didn't drain profits. He then opened a branch store which, utilizing the same techniques, produced almost one half a million dollars in profit over the next five years. All growth came because Sim kept the overhead small and plowed most of the profit back into the business.

9. *Reach For More Wealth The Minute You Hit An Easy Maximum*

If you want to create a big money fortune fast, you must reach for wealth continually. The secret, once you reach the point where your current business product has established itself, is to then start setting cash aside for the next expansion.

Bill H., for instance, began his fortune-building career with $50, a small plot of ground near a medium-sized city and five packages of vegetable seed. The first year he grew corn, tomatoes and squash, built a small stand on the street and sold everything he could grow for $1000 in total income.

The next year he enlarged the operation by buying produce from the neighbors and by building a bigger stand. Within three years his stand covered 100 feet along the street and sold $5000 worth of vegetables a month during the growing season.

Taking this profit nest egg, he next built a small building next door to the vegetable stand and opened a health food restaurant. At this point the health food craze had started, and within four months had pushed the restaurant volume to over $8000 a month.

Bill then decided to try cashing in on the bicycle fad. He rented a small store nearby, bought 75 bicycles and launched the business. The first year this new venture required Bill's undivided attention. After that the operation began to establish itself, and in the third year he sold almost 1500 bicycles. Bill then repeated the process with a small telephone answering service. After that, just as soon as one business got on its feet he opened another. At the end of ten years he was grossing well over $2 million a year from all sources—an overall income that Bill would have never dreamed possible a few years before.

Besides starting separate new businesses as Bill did, it's also possible to begin one business and then expand its functions in many ways as you go along.

John M., for instance, began his fortune-building career by placing poetry on parchment and hanging it in his own home. He received so many favorable comments about this that he decided to market a parchment poem called the "Parents Creed." This item did extremely well. Instead of beginning a separate business, John then added to his line of products a Teen Creed, bean bags, dolls, pajama storage cases, artistic cloth calenders and other items. Each additional item added more income. No sooner had John made one item successful than, he launched another until everything began to work together to produce a really significant income.

Short-cuts, then, should become an integral part of your fortune-building career. Properly utilized, they can expand your fortune-making potential tremendously and make all your time an efficient big money producer.

POINTS TO REMEMBER

1. Try to picture the overall operation and visualize how each piece fits together to complement all others.

2. Save time by checking out several methods at the same time.

3. Make decisions quickly, but change them only after considerable deliberation.

4. Try always to cut down the original asking price.

5. Determine the number of steps needed to accomplish a chore, then try to find alternate methods that will cut needed steps.

6. Be impatient enough with every task to **keep** that task going forward with a vengeance.

7. Turn the tough money decisions over to your subconscious mind.

8. Try to keep all expenses to a minimum.

9. Start expanding the minute an operation becomes self-supporting. Constant expansion will boost you along to a big money fortune almost automatically.

12
Big Growth Opportunities That Pay Off Automatically

Earlier in this book we discussed turning slow cash savings accumulation into fast cash accumulation through business. You can, after that, of course, spend your entire career putting together a big money fortune by simply making your business bigger and bigger until the total cash inflow amounts to millions of dollars each year.

This method is a good one but requires much personal effort and energy on your part. Fortunately, however, as you begin to get along in your fortune-making career, you'll find there is a much easier way to accumulate cash than by working for it. As you progress there will be some point where you will want to stop relying on your own efforts to produce a big money fortune and turn at least part of this job over to your already accumulated cash. Once this happens, you will, of course, expand your millionizing range tremendously.

Use Smart Investment Methods to Pyramid Yourself to a Giant Fortune

As you begin any investment program you will want to follow smart money rules that will make investing itself automatic and keep you on the big money track with as few mistakes as possible. Here are seven general smart money investment tools that will help you zoom ahead to a big money investment fortune:

1. *Set aside money for investment as soon as you can spare $20 a month.*

Always start an investment program the minute you can set aside as little as $20 a month. This will allow you to start building an investment nest egg almost immediately.

To do this, simply establish an easy amount to save. Pay yourself first before paying other bills. If possible, make this payment automatic by authorizing the bank to take the money out of your checking account each month. In this way you will begin to build your investment nest egg painlessly and can swing into action as quickly as possible.

Sid H., a low-paid electronics firm maintenance worker who, for instance, parlayed a $320 investment into a $500,000-a-year water bed business, began his investment program when the business itself had started to gross about $3000 a month. Wanting to take the pressure off himself, he authorized the bank to take a minimum of $20 out of his account each month. When he had accumulated $400 Sam placed a down payment on a half-acre lot worth (at that time) $1500. Within a year the lot value had escalated to $3000. Selling the lot, Sid took this cash profit and invested in a seven-acre parcel on the edge of town worth $7000. Within a year Sid sold this parcel for $35,000. Over the next five years he continued to invest in and sell raw land as it went up in value. At the end of that time his investment fund had grown from the original $400 to well over $180,000.

2. *Review your investment commitment every six months.*

To maximize your big money growth you must look again at your financial condition every six months and see whether or not you can increase your monthly investment savings. Excess cash piling up in your business can be just as harmful to your fortune-building plans as lack of operating cash.

Hal P., for instance, is a dynamic big money fortune builder who turned a $50 nest egg into a seven-million-dollar cosmetics fortune. Early in his career, Hal owned a successful fashion boutique which returned him an estimated $70,000 each year. Hal, of course, continued to expand this business, but for some reason he always had an excess amount of cash. This cash he simply let accumulate in his checking account until at the end of 5 years he had built a $48,000 unused cash balance—completely dead money. At that point Hal took stock of his financial position and realized that the extra cash should be put to work immediately. He then proceeded to place $40,000 in bonds yielding 10 percent interest. This produced $4000 by the end of the next year. At the same time Hal set aside $300 every month from his regular checking account to be utilized for investment purposes. He then took this $7600 and used it as a down payment on a $52,000 duplex. Over the next seven years Hal proceeded to put his investment cash to work in a whole series of investments—from art to apartment houses to office buildings. At the end of that time his investments' value had grown to almost $180,000 dollars—money he would have lost if he had simply been content to let excess money pile up unused in his business checking account.

3. *Start investing the minute you accumulate enough cash to get started.*

The amount needed will vary depending on whether you are investing in the stock market, real estate, art or something else. But whatever you decide, time is money—so you must start at the earliest possible moment.

Warren J., for instance, turned $500 into a $750,000 photo mapping business. Warren began setting aside $20 a month the minute his gross income reached $1000 monthly. After that he regularly increased his investment savings program by an additional $20 a month each time his business showed a $500-a-month volume increase. When Warren accumulated $400 he invested in silver coins, which increased 100 percent in value over the next six months. To this $800 Warren added an additional $120 and purchased industrial bonds which returned 10 percent. By the end of two years his original $400 investment nest egg had increased to almost $1500.

David O., however, who invested $7000 in a fast food restaurant business which soon began to gross over $10,000 a month, had an entirely different story. Since the business itself took most of his time, David O. procrastinated for almost two years, telling himself he'd get around to setting up an investment fund later. At the end of that time, while Warren had already accumulated $1500 in investment cash that he hadn't worked for, David was still thinking about getting started. He had, in effect, literally thrown away money he could have utilized for additional fortune building later on.

4. *Review your investments once every four months.*

It's a cardinal rule in investing that you absolutely must stay on top of your investments just like you do your business. Unfortunately, some investments lose value while others increase. If an investment decreases in value and seems likely to continue to do so in the immediate future, you will want to eliminate that loss quickly. If, however, another investment area has begun to grow and its future looks bright, you will want to invest more cash there before it becomes too costly to make it profitable.

George T., for instance, a retired $9000-a-year Chicago factory worker, built $700 into a $900,000-a-year rental equipment operation. During his second year, George began investing his excess profits. For the next three years he simply put his money—$9000—in the stock market and forgot about it. At the end of that third year, George decided to check on his investment and discovered much to his horror that the total stock portfolio now had an overall value of just $4500—a decline he would have avoided if he had cut his losses quickly.

Noting that everything had lost value except one gold stock, George sold the loser immediately and put the remaining cash in three additional gold stocks. At the end of four months two stocks had gone up and one had gone down. George cashed out the loser and invested in a silver mining firm. This stock increased, but then one of the remaining gold stocks started to decline. George cashed this stock in and reinvested again. By following this procedure over the next two years he regained his $4500 loss besides making a $2000 profit—all because he reviewed his investments regularly and got out of the losers immediately, putting the money into those investments that really performed.

5. *Sell off your poorest performers at least once a year.*

As we've already seen, not all investments will perform at the same rate. While you will always want to review every four months, replacing the losers, there is also no reason you need to retain any investment that isn't performing at its peak. If you want your entire portfolio to produce well, you must also review all investments once a month, selling off the poorest money maker and replacing it with better performers. In this way you will retain only the best investments and keep your money working to its maximum.

Spence B. was a retired $9000-a-year Seattle factory worker before he developed a $900 nest egg into a million dollar food mail order empire. Spence started setting aside investment cash during his second year in the food business. Within three years he had acquired a mutual fund, a duplex, 100 shares of industrial stock, municipal bonds, a small city lot and a few diamonds valued at about $800. For five years Spence left his investments alone, going about his other businesses. At the end of that time their overall value had increased from $1000 to $7500.

Spence decided this just wasn't enough and from then on, decided to drop his worst producer each year and buy something else. At that point he sold off the mutual fund investment and picked up another duplex. The next year he dropped the stock and replaced it with silver bullion. The following year he dropped the first duplex and replaced it with 100 shares of gold stock. As a result his investments during that time increased by $11,000 to 18,500, a gain much over the previous performance.

6. *Sell anything that hasn't increased in value 4 times.*

It may well hurt to sell an outstanding performer, but there's a reason for this rule. Investments generally move in cycles: going up, coming down, increasing rapidly, slowing down and so forth. Playing the smart money odds, any investment that has increased four times over its initial value has probably reached some sort of a peak. Certainly it's possible for it to go higher, but the odds against that increase astronomically the higher the value rises. Therefore, if your investment has increased four times, sell it and then replace the money immediately with another investment having a lower base value. This will give you a greater potential for overall increase.

Bert J. was a Washington State timber operator who got rich almost overnight. Bert utilizes this system regularly to maximize his investment program.

In one case, Bert bought 1000 shares of a stock that increased five times within seven months from $3 to $15 a share. Since this amounted to a more than fourfold increase, Bert decided to sell. He then cashed out, took his $15,000, put $3000 in silver coins and the same amount in raw land. The rest he invested in a small house, a mutual fund and an electronics industry stock. Over the next six months the silver tripled in value, the raw land increased in value to $500 and the house increased in value by $1000. The mutual fund went down $500 and the stock depreciated by $500. Added together, the total value of the investments increased by $8000. The original stock increased to $20 a share and then held steady. If Bert had held this investment he would have realized an additional $5000 over the selling price. By selling and reinvesting in lower priced investments with good potential, however, Bert made $8000. In effect, he got out when the growth of the original investment started to level off, reinvesting the money to obtain greater profit potential.

7. *Set up an investment file.*

To really maximize your investment dollar, you must keep up to date with what's happening to all types of investments and be ready to move at the

right time. This means having the right information
when you need it.

You can do this easily by simply setting up an
investment file. Newspapers like *The Wall Street
Journal* and magazines like *Business Week* frequently
discuss various types of investments.

Your daily newspaper, magazine advertisements,
special investment newsletters, books and other
sources add to the input. Every time you read or hear
something you think you might use, clip it out or jot
yourself a note and pop it in your file; then review
your file every week. Within a short time you will
discover that you are now aware of a great many
more investment opportunities than you'd ever
dreamed existed. You will have accumulated some
information on many of them and have a place from
which to further research investment areas that you
feel warrant exploration.

Stan R., for instance, a former $7000-a-year-
Chicago hardware store clerk, turned a $560 invest-
ment into a five-million-dollar do-it-yourself home
improvement fortune. Stan utilized the investment
file method throughout his entire money-making
career. Stan simply popped anything into the file he
thought he might utilize later. Within six months this
included information on antiques, Chinese art, old
automobiles, scrap steel, Hong Kong imports, used
boats, marinas, rock and roll bands, unusual games, a
gasless automobile and many others.

Intrigued with the energy situation, Stan reviewed
the "gasless automobile" idea and then did extensive
research on the possibilities of alternate energy trans-
port sources. When finished he decided to back the
inventor of a new "gasless" car with $2000. Two
months later the energy crisis struck, interest peaked
and several people offered him $10,000 for his
interest in the invention. Stan sold, took his profit of

$8000 and went on to another investment area. In the meantime, however, gasoline became plentiful again, the bottom dropped out of the gasless car idea and the inventor went broke. Stan, however, still had his $8000 profit, which he would have missed if he had failed to maintain an active investment file.

Look For These Automatic Growth Features In Any Big Money Investment:

1. *A good investment should require only minimum time and effort.*

Buying and remodeling houses is actually an investment but it requires much time and physical work. This ties up time which should be spent in direct business activities. Stock, on the other hand, doesn't require your physical presence. Any increase in the value of a stock after you buy it is unrelated to anything you yourself might do. This makes a good investment (providing the stock market generally is going up), since it allows you to invest your time and energy in other matters while your investment money continues to increase on its own.

Abner H. was a former $8000-a-year Denver supermarket clerk. Abner first built an $800 nest egg into a million-dollar-a-year gross in a retail craft store operation. After that he decided it was time to really start investing. Abner made the decision to put $40,000 into a trailer rental fleet based in the parking lot directly behind his craft store.

This idea worked well during the spring months when he could handle the business volume easily. Then suddenly the summer vacation season broke and Abner found himself handling 500 phone calls a day, sending out 40 to 50 trailers a day and supervising much additional activity. Abner first tried turning the rental operation over to an employee. That didn't work, however, and after the first week he found himself personally handling every detail. As a result, he had to neglect his primary store management responsibilities.

For a while the store squeaked by, but then volume began to drop off as inventory declined. The trailer investment itself took in $19,000 that first summer, but Abner lost $75,000 overall because of the personal time required to launch the trailer operation. The next year he sold the trailers and put the money into bonds returning 10 percent interest. As a result, he netted a $4000 yearly profit and brought the store back to normal volume.

2. *A good investment should have a history of at least doubling in value over the last five years.*

This rule allows you to easily eliminate outdated investment areas. Stocks, for instance, will double and triple at certain times during a five-year period. That, however, hasn't been the history over the last five years. Smart money investors, then will for the moment put their money elsewhere.

James G., a former Seattle factory worker, made a huge fortune in the recreational vehicle business. After his fourth year in business, James felt he ought to put $300 a month in some solid investment area. James chose stocks, and began to investigate several possibilities. His first choice was several electronics firms whose stock value had initially skyrocketed and then leveled off over the last seven years.

Despite this, James went ahead, putting up an initial $7000 and then $300 a month after that. Unfortunately, the stock value remained stagnant over the next 18 months, at which time James sold the stock, took his money and began to look for better investment areas. Noting that land value in his city had continued to increase, James investigated further and discovered that most had doubled over the last five years. He then invested the entire $10,600, utilizing it as a down payment on several parcels. Within two years the $10,600 had increased to almost $21,000, at which time James sold out and went on to other investment areas.

Despite the generally poor investment performance of stocks during the current period, however, certain kinds of stocks have gone wild. Gold stocks, for instance, have shown tremendous growth over the last few years. Anyone buying this kind of stock would have accumulated an excellent profit.

3. *Make sure any investment you buy is in the early stages of growth.*

Gold, for instance, began at $32 an ounce and then jumped to a high of $190 within a very few months. Anyone buying gold during the early stages would have doubled, tripled or quadrupled their money. After that, however, gold leveled off and even declined slightly. Most investment areas behave like this: they start big, make good growth, and then level off. In considering any investment it is vital to get in low on the growth cycle so you have a chance of at least doubling your money.

Walter W. decided to try his luck in land investment. Walter, a big money fortune builder, turned $60 into an apartment house fortune. At the end of his first five years, he bought a two-acre lot in a developed area for $13,000. Two years before speculators had sold the land in five-acre lots for $10,000 each. Buyers constructed several houses, then sold off the remaining lots for $4000 an acre. When Walter purchased his land the value had appreciated to $6500. He then held the lot for two years and sold out for $7000. Disappointed, he put the money back in his investment fund, noting that he had bought almost at the top of the investment cycle.

Walter then vowed to try again at a different level. This time he purchased for $6000 a two-acre lot which had been held for many years in a large ownership parcel. Over the next two years several buyers built large homes nearby. At the end of this time Walter put his two acres up for sale at $60,000. Within three weeks a buyer snapped the lot up—no questions asked—all because Walter had invested this time at the beginning of the land's growth cycle.

4. *Make sure the investment is stable and has good growth potential*

Silver, for instance, has just gone through a growth spurt and seems fairly stable for the near future. Stocks, on the other hand, have gone down for some time and no one can predict when the bear market will end. Any investment in stock (except for selected issues) appears poor until the market turns around.

Bill P., a former $9000-a-year high school teacher, made $1,000,000 in mail order. Bill decided in about his third year in business, to invest some of his profit for future growth.

He put $20,000 in a private suburban area bus service that looked promising. Unfortunately the company faltered and went broke within six months. Taking a closer look, Bill discovered that local private transportation systems everywhere had considerable trouble making a profit and even public systems needed subsidies to keep going.

Bill decided that maybe he should invest next in a proposed new nursing home project. Instead of jumping in this time, however, Bill studied the entire nursing home picture first. He discovered that most private nursing homes were doing extremely well, that the demand had increased tremendously and that the entire industry had become quite stable.

On the basis of this information Bill then invested

an additional $20,000. Within two years, the value of his investment doubled, and a year after that he received a $100,000 offer for his share of the business.

To check this factor for yourself, simply take each investment area you are considering and make a rough determination of how good it appears at the moment. If you need additional information, first consult your local banker for his advice and then investigate at least six similar investments in other localities.

5. *Make sure you can begin your investment program with $500 or less.*

Investments which require large amounts of capital become a definite handicap for the smart money investor who wants to stay flexible. You can, for instance, put your money in equipment (for leasing) like a jet plane, bus or truck, and reap a huge big money profit. This, however, requires a large cash investment and exposes you to considerable loss if anything goes wrong. In addition, you lose considerable flexibility by tying up large amounts of capital and can't move easily from one investment area to another.

Scott R., for instance, an $8000-a-year retired postal clerk, had turned a $700 investment into a $300,000-a-year custom cabinet business. He was offered the chance to invest in land along with several partners.

The investment itself required $40,000 which could not be removed for six years. After thinking it over Scott decided to go ahead and invest every spare dollar. At the end of the first year, a competitor came to him and offered to sell his entire business for $5000. Scott tried to convert the investment back into cash but unfortunately couldn't do it. He didn't have any extra capital available and couldn't borrow an additional penny at that time.

Unfortunately, he had to let the opportunity go by. Another competitor, however, bought the business, and within two years realized a $70,000 profit. Scott lost this profit because he neglected to remain flexible. The rule, then is: Keep initial investments as small as possible. When over $500 is needed, consider each individual investment carefully and go ahead only when the returns appear exceptional.

6. *Make sure you can convert any investment into cash within two months.*

Flexibility is vital as we have seen. You can, of course, simply put your money in an investment and leave it there over an extended period of time. This method may well boost you to riches. More likely, however (as we've already seen), you will miss out on one or more really big money opportunities.

You must, then weigh the different factors carefully. Reasonably priced land in a growth area, for instance, sells rapidly. The more you ask for that land, however (in relation to the going price for similar land), the longer it will take to sell. Land located some distance from major growth areas also will require some time to convert into cash.

Paul F., formerly a $9000-a-year California electronics worker, but recently owner of a rental agency, had turned a spare time operation begun on a $75 shoestring into a three-million-dollar-a-year enterprise. Paul decided, in his fifth year of business, to begin investing in land, and, after searching for six months, fell in love with a small valley containing four small farms 100 miles from the nearest city. He purchased one farm for $65,000 and proceeded to rebuild a small barn for an additional $5000.

At the end of three years Paul had a chance to buy

into a very successful nursery business for $60,000 cash. Not having the money available, he put the farm on the market for $80,000 and waited. Few buyers, however, were interested in that particular area and during the six months Paul had the farm listed, no offers came in. Finally at the end of this period one buyer offered $45,000. By that time the nursery owners had already found another invester.

Paul accepted the offer, however, sold the farm and reinvested the money in vacant land in a nearby growing community. At the end of that year, Paul put that land on the market for $95,000. A buyer bought it for the asking price almost immediately and Paul went on to utilize that cash for other investments.

For all investments you must first consider if you have a ready market for that investment and if you can convert it back into cash easily.

7. *Keep personal control of all investments.*

To maximize your big money potential you must have flexibility. This means you must have complete control of ownership and be able to move fast. With stocks, for instance, you can hold the stock certificates yourself in your name or they can be held for you at your brokerage firm (in their name).

In addition (as mentioned before), many people today make large investments in land, apartment houses, buildings and other kinds of high capital investments in partnership with others. Under this arrangement the partnership contains a managing partner and a number of general partners. The managing partner generally maintains complete control; all others must obtain permission to sell or exchange their ownership and have absolutely no say in the management of their invested money. This leaves you (as a general partner) with little flexibility.

Jepson D., a spare time fortune builder, had built a $300 nest egg into a million dollars a year in used car sales. After several years in the business Jepson put part of his spare cash into large land acreage, along with seven other investors and a managing partner.

Three years after he made the land investment, the owner of a nearby recreational vehicle business offered to sell out to Jepson at a giveaway price. Unfortunately, the managing partner of the land acreage refused to let Jepson sell his interest. As a result, he had to let the recreational vehicle opportunity go for an estimated $3-million-dollar loss over the next three years. This occurred because Jepson failed to retain personal control. The rule, then, is: Whenever possible, avoid any kind of remote ownership and retain complete control of all investments yourself.

Check These Six Big Money Investment Areas:

Here are six red hot big money investment areas you should consider today.

Art

The dollar today has undergone considerable devaluation, yet art just keeps on getting better as an investment opportunity in the face of this situation. Thousands of investors who at one time bought only stocks and bonds are today putting money into art.

Winston B. decided to terminate his stock investments and put some of his spare cash into modern art. Winston, however, knew little about art investing himself, but one of his friends who ran a small gallery agreed to help him invest $2500 in a dozen or so good abstract paintings ranging in price from $150 to $300.

Within a year of the purchase the paintings were appraised at $3500; by the end of the second year $5500, and by the fourth $7500. During the fifth year Winston sold the paintings for $10,000, then turned around and reinvested the money in another art area.

In addition to individual investors, the international art market is booming as never before and businesses such as Westinghouse, Neiman Marcus and others are for the first time putting more and more cash into art as an investment opportunity.

In the art field you will find a tremendous choice of investment areas. Super realism (complete in camera-eye detail) is now in vogue; several artists in this area sell individual paintings for $5000 and up. Prints are also currently appreciating at about 15 percent a year and range in value from $100 to $600.

In general, every area has its favorite artists. Often you can buy the works of talented newcomers at a reasonable price ($100 and up) and ride the rise up.

How do you break in? First you need to learn something about art itself. Visit your local art gallery or museum; pick up any printed material. Ask about techniques and prices; also, put your name on the mailing list for regular bulletins.

Next, read the art section of the local newspaper. Finally (when possible) take an art appreciation course (available through many adult education programs at your local high school), or take out a subscription to one of the magazines in the field: *Art News,* 444 Madison Ave, New York, New York 10022; *Today's Art,* 25 West 45 St. New York, New York 10036.

The real secret of making money in art is to first learn what it's all about, start small ($100 to $250) and then add to your collection carefully as you go along.

Antiques

Antique collecting has today become an important field for individual investors, since prices in general continue to increase at the rate of 10 to 20 percent a year. It's still possible, however, to enter some part of the field for as little as $10 with the average investment running $25 to $700.

Tony H. was a $7000-a-year high school custodian estabblished a small but successful riding stable. Several years ago Tony started putting extra investment cash into old phonographs. He haunted the antique shops everywhere looking for a wide selection of old record-players. Over the years Tony picked up several old phonographs ranging in price from $10 to $260. At the end of ten years he lost interest and called in an antique auctioneer to appraise the collection. Much to Tony's surprise the collection, was appraised for $50,000 and sold at auction for slightly over that amount, an almost tenfold increase in value in ten short years.

Antique collecting today covers a wide range of items: furnitue, books, engravings, bicycles, guns, dolls, Persian rugs, candles and much more.

Start your investing in antiques by reading one of the magazines in the antique field: *Antiques,* 651 Fifth Ave., New York, New York 10017, or *Spinning Wheel,* Hanover, Pennsylvania 17331. Next read several basic books such as *Price Guide to Antiques and Pattern Glass* (Homestead), *Complete Antiques Price List* (Crown), *Practical Guide to Antique Collecting* (Arco). After that, go to a few auctions to get the feel of what's happening; then slowly start out collecting on your own. After a year or two, have your collection appraised by a local gallery or auctioneer, then adjust your collecting in accordance with how much each individual item has appreciated since they were first purchased.

Autographs

Autographs, like many other collectable items today, have an appreciating value and can make money for you as an investment. Currently you can still buy letters, manuscripts, documents and signatures of notables for a modest sum ($1 to $200).

Bill J., a former San Francisco taxi driver, had turned a $300 investment into a $3-million skating rink development. Bill started collecting letters from the heads of state of important foreign countries. He received some during his taxi driving days by simply asking important passengers from the various countries to get them for him. He bought others from collectors around town. Over the years, Bill added notes from Charles De Gaulle to various cabinet members, letters from Franco to members of his family, notes from the Japanese emperor and others.

Much to his surprise, at the end of ten years the collection itself was appraised at value of $20,000.

Autographs themselves cycle in value. Different fields and different people come into favor and then fade. A new movie or a book will drum up interest. Some that currently are in vogue are letters of General Patton and Freud. The value of a letter lies in what it reveals about the writer and his contribution to history. A routine note by Theodore Roosevelt brings $35; a letter discussing Latin American matters, $500. Look for autographs with full signatures rather than initials.

To start, simply decide what kinds of autographs you'd like to collect and then begin. For more information consult *Patterson's Autographs, a Collectors Guide* (Crown), and *Big Name Hunting* (Simon and Schuster). The Antiquarian Booksellers Association of America, 630 Fifth Ave., New York, New York 10020, also publishes a membership list which will help you get started.

Vintages Photographs

Photography today is rapidly becoming big business for art dealers. Prices of photos have risen over the last few years from $100 to as much as $1000. Collectors are buying up the work of outstanding photographers. The most dramatic price increases have occurred with the works of nineteenth-century photographers and modern special interest photographers.

Diane A., for instance, who won fame by photographing helpless, grotesque people, has become extremely popular. Prices for her work increased an astronomical 800 percent in just two years. One investor, for instance, recently bought one of her photographs one day for $185 and sold it two days later for $600.

You can obtain information on values from such art dealers as the Watkin Gallery, 243 East 60 St., New York; the Leigh Gallery, 1018 Madison Ave., New York, and the Museum of Modern Art, 11 West 53 St., New York.

Start by selecting two or three photographers that appeal for you; then search for their work in antique shops, art galleries and similar places. You can generally pick up photographs at prices ranging from $1 to $15.

Jewelry

Jewelry today is one of the hottest big money investment fields around. Jewelry currently appreciates from 10 to 20 percent a year. There many types to choose from: African jewelry, American Indian jewelry, Egyptian jewelry, gold, diamonds, rubies, and many more.

Thelma M., a former Ohio school teacher, turned a $600 nest egg into a six-store franchise shop operation. Thelma determined from the beginning to buy diamonds whenever she could spare an extra dollar or two for investment. Over the years she managed to save about $15,000, all of which she put into various types of diamond purchases—rings, necklaces, a bracelet, etc. At the time she wasn't aware of the tremendous value increase in diamonds, but at the end of ten years, her $15,000 investment was appraised at $40,000—all without any effort on her part.

To start your own jewelry investment, contact a reputable jeweler (see the telephone yellow pages), explain what you have in mind and get his advice. In addition, start collecting information and material wherever you find it; then slowly start to put your own collection together.

Coin Collecting

Coin collecting as an investment offers probably more opportunity today than ever before. Over the last 10 years, for instance, the value of many individual coins has risen an astounding 3000 percent. In addition, the U.S. Coinage Act of 1965 has in itself begun to force up the price of older silver coins, since the act in effect took silver coins out of circulation and replaced them with a coin containing 40 percent less silver. Many of these earlier silver coins still remain in circulation, making it possible to pick them up at face value and then cash in on the increase in value as they become scarce.

Martin Ready, for instance, a former $10,000-a-year New York bus driver who parlayed $700 into a three-million-dollar-a-year motel empire, began during his second year in business to build an investment coin collection. He initially studied several books and then took an adult education class in coin collecting. After that he simply began to collect. Within two years he had picked up coins worth almost $15,000 (several of his coins had a value of almost $1000 each). Within five years the collection had grown to an appraised value of $40,000, largely on the basis of Martin's knowledge and constant search for good coins which he knew would increase in value.

What Martin did, of course, you can do too. For more information on coin collecting as an investment, consult the book *Secrets of a Professional Coin Dealer,* Fred and Abner Benson (Pocket Books).

Start your own investing by selecting the types of coins you want to collect. After that, look for them by buying rolls of coins from the bank, trade with other collectors for the ones you want, or purchase them from coin dealers located through the telephone book yellow pages.

How To Decide Which Fortune-Making Investments Will Work For You

While investments alone will keep your dollars working, it's extremely important to match your investments to your personality and program. To keep on maximizing your investment return at all times, you must make all your energy forces work for you in positive direction. Here are the factors you'll want to consider.

1. *Consider the preparation necessary.* Some investment areas require a great deal of expertize. In art, for instance, you must do a great deal of homework before you become qualified to decide which paintings offer a good investment opportunity and which do not.

Regan H., for instance, a Seattle fortune builder who parlayed a $50 nest egg into a $100,000-a-year real estate income, decided to invest some of his spare cash in art. The question was—which art? Regan first went to a local art gallery and asked how he should go about starting a personal collection. The answer was to pick a specialty and then immerse himself in the subject. He began to subscribe to several art magazines, got on the mailing list of several large museums, took a course in art appreciation and asked for catalogues from several big art dealers (found in large city phone books). He then began to clip every piece of art information he could find in his chosen field of oriental art.

After a while he began to understand why collectors considered some paintings valuable and not others. By the end of the year he had picked up 15 paintings for $5000. These doubled in value within two years.

Regan, however, estimated he had spent at least ten hours a week the first year simply doing the necessary legwork. The same study, time and commitment are necessary in almost every other investment area, including stocks, bonds, mutual funds and similar investments. Some, of course, simply take more work than others.

The general rule is: read several books on your chosen investment area, then decide what you will need to do to pick up the neccessary expertise. After that, proceed to acquire the information necessary to make yourself a successful investor in that area.

2. *Consider the total time involved.* Besides preparation time, some investments require a certain amount of handling time. If you are active in the stock market, for instance, you will need to spend certain amounts of time on the phone, in reading about investments, on paperwork and on other details.

With art, you need to invest a certain amount of time in upkeep. While most investment won't take large amounts of time, you should consider this factor initially. Here are a few investment areas with some additional time needs:

Stocks:
> handling individual transactions
> following the market daily

Mutual funds:
> buying and selling transactions
> studying individual funds

Real estate (land):
> looking for land
> getting water, power, etc. to the land
> showing the land to prospective purchasers
> additional paperwork

Art, antiques, autographs and similar hobbies:
> keeping up the collection
> going to shows
> additional paperwork

To decide how much time your own investment area will take, simply list all tasks, estimate the time needed, and then add up the total. After that, decide if you can handle the proposed investment in the time you have available.

3. *Consider how much money you intend to invest.* You have already established an investment savings

plan and are now accumulating money, of course. You should at this point, then, try to match your available money to your investment. With art, for instance you will often invest as much as $500 or more for a single painting. Mutual funds and stocks can be accumulated for as little as $20 a month. Whatever you do, simply try to equate the amount saved with the cash needed.

Brent Rampton, for instance, a retired teacher who turned a $300 nest egg into a fortune selling Eskimo crafts, decided to invest in vintage antique cars. At this point, however, Brent began to run short of cash, yet each car he tried to buy required a minimum of $18,000. As a result, he purchased only inferior cars which failed to appreciate in value over the next year. At the end of this time Brent re-evaluated his investment program in the light of the available cash and decided to return to a standard stock program which more closely matched his needs.

4. *Consider your future plans.* Some investments fit your plans and present business well; others don't. Rick Hamilton, for instance, planned over the next five years to build a chain of restaurants in a six-state area. To do this effectively he bought a motor home and equipped it as a roving office. At the same time, he also started to invest heavily in art. After a few years on the road Rick returned home so seldom that he decided to sell his house and live full time in the motor home.

Rick no longer had display space for the paintings and had to pay extra for storage. As a result, he sold the paintings within a few months and invested in art-oriented stock instead. While not as interesting an investment, the stock allowed him to travel without the problems of a large art collection.

To match your investment to your business, simply lay out your future tentatively over the next five years; then ask yourself if your proposed investment area fits well with what you're planning. If not, change directions and explore other types of investments.

5. *Consider Your Own Interests.* It is extremely important that you enjoy the investment area you are about to enter. James H., for instance, loved sports but when it came time to invest he put his money in stocks because all his friends insisted. Instead of studying the market carefully, however, James ignored all common sense and bought helter skelter whenever a company struck his fancy. After six years the stocks themselves were worth about $3000 less than their original purchase value. At this point James sold his entire portfolio and put the money into a new sports complex about to be constructed in his city. He became extremely interested in the sports complex plans, attended all meetings, offered valuable suggestions and generally stayed on top of what was happening. Within two years James' investment doubled. When he finally cashed out 12 years later, his original $11,000 had grown to over $92,000.

Chart Your Big Money Investment Profits

With all investments, you should have some visual way of knowing just how well each investment performs. This will alert you almost immediately to any change in your investment progress.

Simply take a piece of paper and mark the lower edge equally into the months of the year starting with the present month (May, June, July, etc.) Then mark the left hand edge of your paper to represent the value of your investment. If you have purchased paintings worth $10,000, for instance, the values marked on the left hand edge should range from $5000 to about $20,000.

When you begin your investment program, mark the

estimated value on the chart at that point; then re-estimate the value each month and enter it on the chart. After a few months, connect all the points with a thick pencil or crayon and take a look at what's happening. This will give you a visual record of where you are at all times and allow you to take any necessary action.

POINTS TO REMEMBER

Investments allow spare cash to earn extra money with a minimum effort on your part.

Follow these rules to a big money investment:

1. Set aside money for investment the minute you can spare $20 a month.

2. Review your investment commitment every six months.

3. Start investing the minute you accumulate enough cash to get started.

4. Review your investments once every four months.

5. Sell off the poorest performers at least once a year.

6. Sell any investment that hasn't increased in value four times.

7. Set up an investment file.

Make sure:

1. That you perform minimum work with any cash investment.

2. That the general investment area has doubled over the last five years.

3. That the investment itself is in the early stages of growth.

4. That the investment has good growth potential.

5. That the investment can be easily converted to cash.

6. That you retain personal control of investments at all times.

Besides regular investment areas consider: art, autographs, antiques, coins, jewelry and vintage photographs.

Consider:

1. The amount of preparation needed.

2. The necessary time involved.

3. The cash needed for particular investments.

4. Your future plans.

5. Your own general interests.

INDEX